GOLF RULES ILLUSTRATED

TENTH EDITION

COMPILED BY
THE ROYAL AND ANCIENT GOLF CLUB OF ST ANDREWS

ILLUSTRATIONS BY
**PETER DAVIDSON
AND HELIX DESIGN PARTNERSHIP**

Foreword

I welcome the opportunity to introduce the tenth *Golf Rules Illustrated*.

In common with previous editions, this popular publication incorporates the current Rules of Golf, which the R&A continues to make available in booklet form free of charge through a partnership with Royal & SunAlliance since 1908.

The excellent colour illustrations show how to apply the Rules properly in many different situations, but what sets this particular edition apart from its predecessors is the inclusion, for the first time, of a number of examples of Rules incidents in tournament play. The cover incident in which Tiger Woods' ball came to rest close to a large loose impediment in the desert course in Scottsdale, Arizona is now well known, but where in the Rules does it actually permit him to have it removed?

The answer to this question – and other celebrated Rules queries – are to be found within these pages.

Irrespective of how well you play golf, there is no doubt that a good working knowledge of the Rules adds to the satisfaction of the game and I know you will find that this book helps to bring the Rules of Golf alive. I am sure you will enjoy it.

IAN R. H. PATTINSON
Chairman, Rules of Golf Committee,
Royal & Ancient Golf Club of St. Andrews

This edition produced in 2002 for The Book People Ltd,
Hall Wood Avenue, Haydock, St Helens, WA11 9UL

Published in 2001
by Hamlyn, a division of Octopus Publishing Group Ltd
2–4 Heron Quays, London E14 4JP

Text copyright © 2001 Royal & Ancient Golf Club
Design copyright © 2001 Octopus Publishing Group Ltd

ISBN 0 600 60629 5

A CIP catalogue record for this book is available from the British Library

Printed in Italy

10 9 8 7 6 5 4 3 2

CONTENTS

SECTION 1
ETIQUETTE

COURTESY ON THE COURSE

Safety: Prior to playing a stroke or making a practice swing, the player should ensure that no one is standing close by or in a position to be hit by the club, the ball or any stones, pebbles, twigs or the like which may be moved by the stroke or swing.

Consideration for Other Players: The player who has the honour should be allowed to play before his opponent or fellow-competitor tees his ball.

No one should move, talk or stand close to or directly behind the ball or the hole when a player is addressing the ball or making a stroke.

No player should play until the players in front are out of range.

Pace of Play: In the interest of all, players should play without delay.

If a player believes his ball may be lost outside a water hazard or out of bounds, to save time, he should play a provisional ball.

Players searching for a ball should signal the players behind them to pass as soon as it becomes apparent that the ball will not easily be found. They should not search for five minutes before doing so. They should not continue play until the players following them have passed and are out of range.

When the play of a hole has been completed, players should immediately leave the putting green.

If a match fails to keep its place on the course and loses more than one clear hole on the players in front, it should invite the match following to pass.

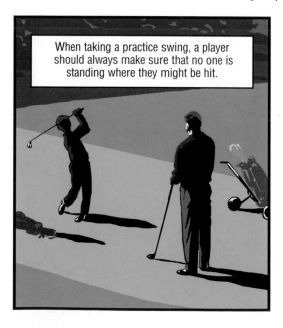

When taking a practice swing, a player should always make sure that no one is standing where they might be hit.

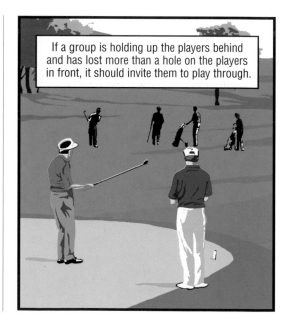

If a group is holding up the players behind and has lost more than a hole on the players in front, it should invite them to play through.

PRIORITY ON THE COURSE

In the absence of special rules, two-ball matches should have precedence over and be entitled to pass any three- or four-ball match, which should invite them through.

A single player has no standing and should give way to a match of any kind.
Any match playing a whole round is entitled to pass a match playing a shorter round.

CARE OF THE COURSE

Holes in Bunkers: Before leaving a bunker, a player should carefully fill up and smooth over all holes and footprints made by him.

Repair Divots, Ball-Marks and Damage by Spikes: A player should ensure that any divot hole made by him and any damage to the putting green made by a ball is carefully repaired. **On completion of the hole** by all players in the group, damage to the putting green caused by golf shoe spikes should be repaired.

Damage to Greens — Flagsticks, Bags, etc: Players should ensure that, when putting down bags or the flagstick, no damage is done to the putting green and that neither they nor their caddies damage the hole by standing close to it, in handling the flagstick or in removing the ball from the hole. The flagstick should be properly replaced in the hole before the players leave the putting green. Players should not damage the putting green by leaning on their putters, particularly when removing the ball from the hole.

Golf Carts: Local notices regulating the movement of golf carts should be strictly observed.

Damage Through Practice Swings: In taking practice swings, players should avoid causing damage to the *course*, particularly the tees, by removing divots.

Always repair divots (top right), carefully repair pitch marks on the putting green (bottom left) and smooth over footprints and other marks when leaving a bunker (bottom centre). Do not lean on your putter when removing the ball from the hole (middle right).

SECTION 2
DEFINITIONS

The Definitions are placed in alphabetical order and some are also repeated at the beginning of their relevant Rule.
In the Rules themselves, defined terms which may be important to the application of a Rule are set in italics the first time they appear.

ADDRESSING THE BALL

Except in a hazard, a player has addressed the ball when he has taken his stance and grounded his club.

In a bunker or water hazard a player has addressed the ball when he has taken his stance.

The player has decided not to ground his putter. Therefore, he has not "addressed the ball" and cannot be penalised under Rule 18-2b.

Abnormal Ground Conditions: An "abnormal ground condition" is any *casual water, ground under repair* or hole, cast or runway on the *course* made by a *burrowing animal,* a reptile or a bird.

Addressing the Ball: A player has "addressed the ball" when he has taken his *stance* and has also grounded his club, except that in a *hazard* a player has addressed the ball when he has taken his stance.

Advice: "Advice" is any counsel or suggestion which could influence a player in determining his play, the choice of a club or the method of making a *stroke*.

Information on the *Rules* or on matters of public information, such as the position of *hazards* or the *flagstick* on the *putting green*, is not advice.

Ball Deemed to Move: See "Move or Moved."

Ball Holed: See "Holed."

Ball Lost: See "Lost Ball."

Ball in Play: A ball is "in play" as soon as the player has made a *stroke* on the *teeing ground*. It remains in play until holed out, except when it is *lost, out of bounds* or lifted, or another ball has been substituted whether or not such substitution is permitted; a ball so substituted becomes the ball in play.

Bunker: A "bunker" is a *hazard* consisting of a prepared area of ground, often a hollow, from which turf or soil has been removed and replaced with sand or the like. Grass-covered ground bordering or within a bunker is not part of the bunker. The margin of a bunker extends vertically downwards, but not upwards. A ball is in a bunker when it lies in or any part of it touches the bunker.

Burrowing Animal: A "burrowing animal" is an animal that makes a hole for habitation or shelter, such as a rabbit, mole,

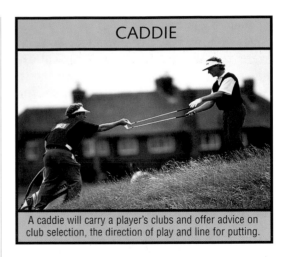

CADDIE

A caddie will carry a player's clubs and offer advice on club selection, the direction of play and line for putting.

ground hog, gopher or salamander.

Note: A hole made by a non-burrowing animal, such as a dog, is not an *abnormal ground condition* unless marked or declared as *ground under repair*.

Caddie: A "caddie" is one who carries or handles a player's clubs during play and otherwise assists him in accordance with the *Rules*.

When one caddie is employed by more than one player, he is always deemed to be the caddie of the player whose ball is involved, and *equipment* carried by him is deemed to be that player's *equipment*, except when the caddie acts upon specific directions of another player, in which case he is considered to be that other player's caddie.

Casual Water: "Casual water" is any

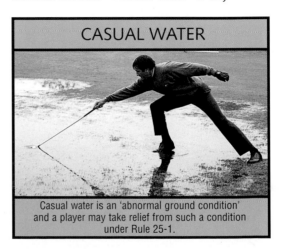

CASUAL WATER

Casual water is an 'abnormal ground condition' and a player may take relief from such a condition under Rule 25-1.

temporary accumulation of water on the *course* which is visible before or after the player takes his *stance* and is not in a *water hazard*. Snow and natural ice, other than frost, are either casual water or *loose impediments*, at the option of the player. Manufactured ice is an *obstruction*. Dew and frost are not casual water. A ball is in casual water when it lies in or any part of it touches the casual water.

Committee: The "Committee" is the committee in charge of the competition or, if the matter does not arise in a competition, the committee in charge of the *course*.

Competitor: A "competitor" is a player in a stroke competition. A "fellow-competitor" is any person with whom the competitor plays. Neither is *partner* of the other.
 In stroke play foursome and four-ball competitions, where the context so admits, the word "competitor" or "fellow-competitor" includes his partner.

Course: The "course" is the whole area within which play is permitted (see Rule 33-2).

Equipment: "Equipment" is anything used, worn or carried by or for the player except any ball he has played at the hole being played and any small object, such as a coin or a tee, when used to mark the position of a ball or the extent of an area in which a ball is to be dropped. Equipment includes a golf cart, whether or not motorised. If such a cart is shared by two or more players, the cart and everything in it are deemed to be the equipment of the player whose ball is involved except that, when the cart is being moved by one of the players sharing it, the cart and everything in it are deemed to be that player's equipment.
Note: A ball played at the hole being played is equipment when it has been lifted and not put back into play.

Fellow-Competitor: See "Competitor."

Flagstick: The "flagstick" is a movable straight indicator, with or without bunting or

EQUIPMENT

Equipment includes a golf cart. As it is not being moved by one of the players, the cart and everything in it are deemed to be the equipment of the player whose ball is involved.

other material attached, centered in the hole to show its position. It shall be circular in cross-section.

Forecaddie: A "forecaddie" is one who is employed by the *Committee* to indicate to players the position of balls during play. He is an *outside agency*.

Ground Under Repair: "Ground under repair" is any part of the *course* so marked by order of the *Committee* or so declared by its authorised representative. It includes material piled for removal and a hole made by a greenkeeper, even if not so marked.
 All ground and any grass, bush, tree or other growing thing within the ground under repair is part of the ground under repair. The margin of ground under repair extends vertically downwards, but not upwards. Stakes and lines defining ground under repair are in such ground. Such stakes are *obstructions*. A ball is in ground under repair when it lies in or any part of it touches the ground under repair.
Note 1: Grass cuttings and other material left on the *course* which have been abandoned

and are not intended to be removed are not ground under repair unless so marked.

Note 2: The *Committee* may make a Local Rule prohibiting play from ground under repair or an environmentally-sensitive area which has been defined as ground under repair.

Hazards: A "hazard" is any *bunker* or *water hazard*.

Hole: The "hole" shall be 4 1/4 inches (108mm) in diameter and at least 4 inches (100mm) deep. If a lining is used, it shall be sunk at least 1 inch (25mm) below the *putting green* surface unless the nature of the soil makes it impracticable to do so; its outer diameter shall not exceed 4 1/4 inches (108mm).

Holed: A ball is "holed" when it is at rest within the circumference of the *hole* and all of it is below the level of the lip of the hole.

Honour: The player who is to play first from the *teeing ground* is said to have the "*honour.*"

Lateral Water Hazard: A "lateral water hazard" is a *water hazard* or that part of a water hazard so situated that it is not possible or is deemed by the *Committee* to be impracticable to drop a ball behind the water hazard in accordance with Rule 26-1b.

That part of a water hazard to be played as a lateral water hazard should be distinctively marked. A ball is in a lateral water hazard when it lies in or any part of it touches the lateral water hazard.

Note 1: Lateral water hazards should be defined by red stakes or lines.

Note 2: The *Committee* may make a Local Rule prohibiting play from an environmentally-sensitive area which has been defined as a lateral water hazard.

Note 3: The *Committee* may define a lateral water hazard as a water hazard.

Line of Play: The "line of play" is the direction which the player wishes his ball to take after a *stroke*, plus a reasonable distance on either side of the intended direction. The line of play extends vertically upwards from the ground, but does not extend beyond the *hole*.

Line of Putt: The "line of putt" is the line which the player wishes his ball to take after a *stroke* on the *putting green*. Except with respect to Rule 16-1e, the line of putt includes a reasonable distance on either side of the intended line. The line of putt does not extend beyond the *hole*.

Loose Impediments: "Loose impediments" are natural objects such as stones, leaves, twigs, branches and the like, dung, worms and insects and casts or heaps made by them, provided they are not fixed or growing, are not solidly embedded and do not adhere to the ball.

Sand and loose soil are loose impediments on the *putting green*, but not elsewhere.

Snow and natural ice, other than frost, are either *casual water* or loose impediments, at the option of the player. Manufactured ice is an *obstruction*.

Dew and frost are not loose impediments.

Lost Ball: A ball is "*lost*" if:
a. It is not found or identified as his by the player within five minutes after the player's *side* or his or their *caddies* have begun to search for it; or
b. The player has put another ball into play under the *Rules*, even though he may not have searched for the original ball; or
c. The player has played any *stroke* with a *provisional ball* from the place where the original ball is likely to be or from a point nearer the hole than that place, whereupon the provisional ball becomes the *ball in play*.

Time spent in playing a *wrong ball* is not counted in the five-minute period allowed for search.

LOOSE IMPEDIMENTS

Natural objects such as:

branches

stones

dead rat

worm casts

pine cones

leaves

insects

MOVABLE OBSTRUCTIONS

Artificial/manufactured objects such as:

tin can

tee

booklet

rake

litter

bottle

score card

BALL DEEMED TO MOVE

This ball is deemed not to have 'moved' because, having left its original position, it rolled back into it again.

This ball is deemed to have 'moved' because it has left its original position and come to rest in another place; the fact that it has moved vertically, rather than laterally, is irrelevant.

Marker: A "marker" is one who is appointed by the *Committee* to record a *competitor*'s score in stroke play. He may be a *fellow-competitor*. He is not a *referee*.

Matches: See "Sides and Matches."

Move or Moved: A ball is deemed to have "moved" if it leaves its position and comes to rest in any other place.

Nearest Point of Relief: The "nearest point of relief" is the reference point for taking relief without penalty from interference by an immovable *obstruction* (Rule 24-2), an *abnormal ground condition* (Rule 25-1) or a *wrong putting green* (Rule 25-3).

It is the point on the *course*, nearest to where the ball lies, which is not nearer the hole and at which, if the ball were so positioned, no interference (as defined) would exist.

Note: The player should determine his nearest point of relief by using the club with which he expects to play his next stroke to simulate the address position and swing for such stroke.

Observer: An "observer" is one who is appointed by the *Committee* to assist a *referee* to decide questions of fact and to report to him any breach of a *Rule*. An observer should not attend the flagstick, stand at or mark the position of the hole, or lift the ball or mark its position.

Obstructions: An "obstruction" is anything artificial, including the artificial surfaces and sides of roads and paths and manufactured ice, except:

a. Objects defining *out of bounds*, such as walls, fences, stakes and railings;

b. Any part of an immovable artificial object which is *out of bounds*; and

OBSTRUCTIONS

Movable or immovable?

building

tin can

rake

booklet

An obstruction is movable if it may be moved without unreasonable effort, undue delay and causing damage i.e. the tin can, rake, booklet and hose.

standpipe and hose

11

c. Any construction declared by the *Committee* to be an integral part of the course.

An obstruction is a movable obstruction if it may be moved without unreasonable effort, without unduly delaying play and without causing damage. Otherwise it is an immovable obstruction.

Note: The *Committee* may make a Local Rule declaring a movable obstruction to be an immovable obstruction.

Out of Bounds: "Out of bounds" is beyond the boundaries of the *course* or any part of the course so marked by the *Committee*.

When out of bounds is defined by reference to stakes or a fence or as being beyond stakes or a fence, the out of bounds line is determined by the nearest inside points of the stakes or fence posts at ground level excluding angled supports.

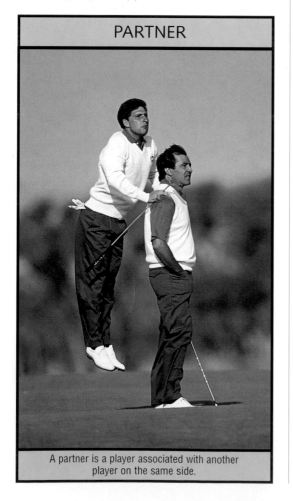

PARTNER

A partner is a player associated with another player on the same side.

Objects defining out of bounds such as walls, fences, stakes and railings, are not *obstructions* and are deemed to be fixed.

When out of bounds is defined by a line on the ground, the line itself is out of bounds.

The out of bounds line extends vertically upwards and downwards.

A ball is out of bounds when all of it lies out of bounds.

A player may stand out of bounds to play a ball lying within bounds.

Outside Agency: An "outside agency" is any agency not part of the match or, in stroke play, not part of the competitor's *side*, and includes a *referee*, a *marker*, an *observer* and a *forecaddie*. Neither wind nor water is an outside agency.

Partner: A "partner" is a player associated with another player on the same *side*.
In a threesome, foursome, best-ball or four-ball match, where the context so admits, the word "player" includes his partner or partners.

Penalty Stroke: A "penalty stroke" is one added to the score of a player or *side* under certain Rules. In a threesome or foursome, penalty strokes do not affect the order of play.

Provisional Ball: A "provisional ball" is a ball played under Rule 27-2 for a ball which may be *lost* outside a *water hazard* or may be *out of bounds*.

Putting Green: The "putting green" is all ground of the hole being played which is specially prepared for putting or otherwise defined as such by the *Committee*. A ball is on the putting green when any part of it touches the putting green.

Referee: A "referee" is one who is appointed by the *Committee* to accompany players to decide questions of fact and apply the *Rules*. He shall act on any breach of a Rule which he observes or is reported to him.

A referee should not attend the flagstick, stand at or mark the position of the hole, or lift the ball or mark its position.

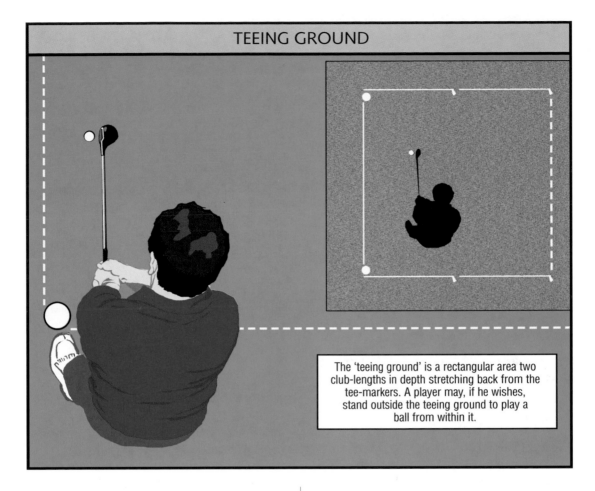

TEEING GROUND

The 'teeing ground' is a rectangular area two club-lengths in depth stretching back from the tee-markers. A player may, if he wishes, stand outside the teeing ground to play a ball from within it.

Rub of the Green: A "rub of the green" occurs when a ball in motion is accidentally deflected or stopped by any *outside agency* (see Rule 19-1).

Rule or Rules: The term "Rule" includes:
a. The Rules of Golf;
b. Any Local Rules made by the *Committee* under Rule 33-8a and Appendix I; and
c. The specifications on clubs and the ball in Appendices II and III.

Sides and Matches:
Side: A player, or two or more players who are *partners*.
Single: A match in which one plays against another.
Threesome: A match in which one plays against two, and each side plays one ball.
Foursome: A match in which two play against two, and each side plays one ball.
Three-Ball: A match play competition in which three play against one another, each playing his own ball. Each player is playing two distinct matches.
Best-Ball: A match in which one plays against the better ball of two or the best ball of three players.
Four-Ball: A match in which two play their better ball against the better ball of two other players.

Stance: Taking the "stance" consists in a player placing his feet in position for and preparatory to making a *stroke*.

Stipulated Round: The "stipulated round" consists of playing the holes of the *course* in their correct sequence unless otherwise authorised by the *Committee*. The number of holes in a stipulated round is 18 unless a smaller number is authorised by the Committee. As to extension of stipulated round in match play, see Rule 2-3.

DEFINITION OF A STROKE

At this point, as the player has not started his downswing, he has not begun his stroke. Once the player begins his downswing he is considered to have made a stroke, unless he checks his downswing voluntarily.

Stroke: A "stroke" is the forward movement of the club made with the intention of fairly striking at and moving the ball, but if a player checks his downswing voluntarily before the clubhead reaches the ball he is deemed not to have made a stroke.

Teeing Ground: The "teeing ground" is the starting place for the hole to be played. It is a rectangular area two club-lengths in depth, the front and the sides of which are defined by the outside limits of two tee-markers. A ball is outside the teeing ground when all of it lies outside the teeing ground.

Through the Green: "Through the green" is the whole area of the *course* except:
a. The *teeing ground* and *putting green* of the hole being played; and
b. All *hazards* on the course.

Water Hazard: A "water hazard" is any sea, lake, pond, river, ditch, surface drainage ditch or other open water course (whether or not containing water) and anything of a similar nature.

All ground or water within the margin of a water hazard is part of the water hazard. The margin of a water hazard extends vertically upwards and downwards. Stakes and lines defining the margins of water hazards are in the hazards. Such stakes are *obstructions*. A ball is in a water hazard when it lies in or any part of it touches the water hazard.
Note 1: Water hazards (other than *lateral water hazards*) should be defined by yellow stakes or lines.
Note 2: The *Committee* may make a Local Rule prohibiting play from an environmentally-sensitive area which has been defined as a water hazard.

Wrong Ball: A "wrong ball" is any ball other than the player's:
a. *Ball in play*,
b. *Provisional ball*, or
c. Second ball played under Rule 3-3 or Rule 20-7b in stroke play.
Note: Ball in play includes a ball substituted for the ball in play whether or not such substitution is permitted.

Wrong Putting Green: A "wrong putting green" is any *putting green* other than that of the hole being played. Unless otherwise prescribed by the *Committee*, this term includes a practice putting green or pitching green on the *course*.

SECTION 3
THE RULES OF PLAY

RULE **1** | ## THE GAME

1-1 GENERAL
The Game of Golf consists in playing a ball from the *teeing ground* into the *hole* by a *stroke* or successive strokes in accordance with the *Rules*.

1-2 EXERTING INFLUENCE ON BALL
No player or caddie shall take any action to influence the position or the movement of a ball except in accordance with the *Rules*.
(Removal of movable obstructions — see Rule 24-1.)

PENALTY FOR BREACH OF RULE 1-2:
Match play — Loss of hole; Stroke play — Two strokes.

Note: In the case of a serious breach of Rule 1-2, the *Committee* may impose a penalty of disqualification.

1-3 AGREEMENT TO WAIVE RULES
Players shall not agree to exclude the operation of any *Rule* or to waive any penalty incurred.

PENALTY FOR BREACH OF RULE 1-3:
Match play — Disqualification of both sides;
Stroke play — Disqualification of competitors concerned.

(Agreeing to play out of turn in stroke play — see Rule 10-2c.)

MATCH PLAY: AGREEMENT TO CONSIDER HOLE HALVED

15

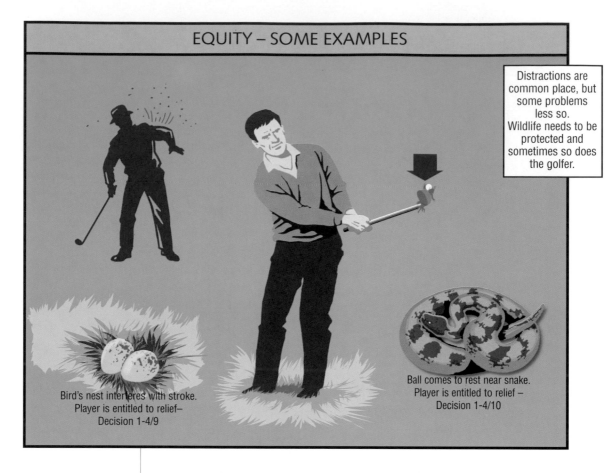

EQUITY – SOME EXAMPLES

Distractions are common place, but some problems less so. Wildlife needs to be protected and sometimes so does the golfer.

Bird's nest interferes with stroke. Player is entitled to relief– Decision 1-4/9

Ball comes to rest near snake. Player is entitled to relief – Decision 1-4/10

See **incident** involving Rule 1-4 below

1-4 POINTS NOT COVERED BY RULES

If any point in dispute is not covered by the *Rules,* the decision shall be made in accordance with equity.

RULE 1 INCIDENT

During the 1990 Dunhill Cup at St. Andrews, on the 17th hole of the final, Mark James hit his second stroke onto the road behind the green. Philip Walton, James' fellow-competitor, hit his approach into the famous "Road Hole" bunker.

While James was preparing for his third stroke from the road, Walton stepped into the bunker to assess his next stroke. Due to the nature of the stroke from the road, James felt it was possible that he might over hit his third stroke. The likely result being that the ball would finish in the bunker, he was concerned that the footprints made by Walton in the bunker may have an adverse effect on his lie.

At this point James sought clarification from a Rules official as to whether he could have Walton's footprints raked. The referee ruled, in equity (Rule 1-4), that James could have the bunker raked, thereby restoring it to its former condition as the footprints had been created by Walton after James' ball had come to rest on the road. As a result of this incident, Decision 13-2/29.5 was introduced in the Decisions on the Rules of Golf.

RULE | MATCH PLAY

2-1 WINNER OF HOLE; RECKONING OF HOLES

In match play the game is played by holes.

Except as otherwise provided in the *Rules*, a hole is won by the side which holes its ball in the fewer strokes. In a handicap match the lower net score wins the hole.

The reckoning of holes is kept by the terms: so many "holes up" or "all square," and so many "to play."

A side is "dormie" when it is as many holes up as there are holes remaining to be played.

2-2 HALVED HOLE

A hole is halved if each side holes out in the same number of strokes.

When a player has holed out and his opponent has been left with a stroke for the half, if the player thereafter incurs a penalty, the hole is halved.

2-3 WINNER OF MATCH

A match (which consists of a *stipulated round*, unless otherwise decreed by the *Committee*) is won by the side which is leading by a number of holes greater than the number of holes remaining to be played.

The Committee may, for the purpose of settling a tie, extend the stipulated round to as many holes as are required for a match to be won.

WINNER OF MATCH: HOLE-BY-HOLE PLAY-OFF

Good putt. That squares the match. We'll have to go back to the 1st for a sudden death play-off.

No. We started this match at the 10th hole, so that is our first extra hole. As before you'll get your handicap stroke.

See **incident** involving Rule 2-4 on page 19

2-4 CONCESSION OF NEXT STROKE, HOLE OR MATCH

When the opponent's ball is at rest or is deemed to be at rest under Rule 16-2, the player may concede the opponent to have holed out with his next *stroke* and the ball may be removed by either side with a club or otherwise.

A player may concede a hole or a match at any time prior to the conclusion of the hole or the match.

Concession of a stroke, hole or match may not be declined or withdrawn.

2-5 CLAIMS

In match play, if a doubt or dispute arises between the players and no duly authorised representative of the *Committee* is available within a reasonable time, the players shall continue the match without delay. Any claim, if it is to be considered by the Committee, must be made before any player in the match plays from the next *teeing ground* or, in the case of the last hole of the match, before all players in the match leave the *putting green*.

No later claim shall be considered unless it is based on facts previously unknown to the player making the claim and the player making the claim had been given wrong information (Rules 6-2a and 9) by an opponent. In any case, no later claim shall be considered after the result of the match has been officially announced, unless the Committee is satisfied that the opponent knew he was giving wrong information.

2-6 GENERAL PENALTY

The penalty for a breach of a *Rule* in match play is loss of hole except when otherwise provided.

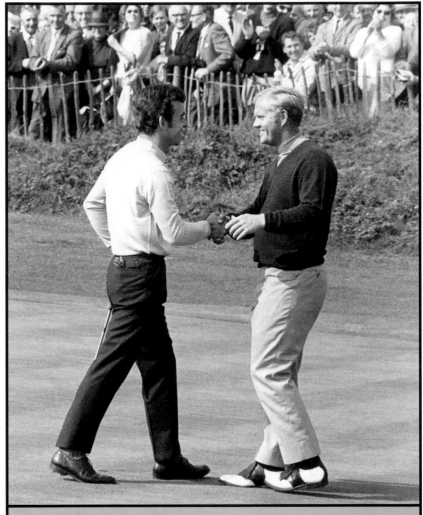

Tony Jacklin and Jack Nicklaus shake hands on the 18th green during the 1969 Ryder Cup.

RULE 2 INCIDENT

Jack Nicklaus' concession of Tony Jacklin's putt on the final hole during the final match of the 1969 Ryder Cup resulted in the event's first tie, and is hailed as one of golf's finest acts of sportsmanship.

Going into the final day's competition at Royal Birkdale Golf Club in Southport, England, the United States and Great Britain and Ireland were even at eight points apiece. That morning's singles matches resulted in a two-point lead for Great Britain and Ireland but the U.S. responded in the afternoon to leave the matches tied at 15½ points each with only the final match of Nicklaus and Jacklin still on the course. Eighteen of the 32 Ryder Cup matches went to the final hole that year, and it was there that the three-day competition would be ultimately decided.

Nicklaus seemed to have the upper hand as Jacklin fell behind on the back nine but the reigning Open champion Jacklin, would not relent. Indeed, he eagled the 17th to go all square with Nicklaus.

19

At the par-5 18th, Jacklin missed his putt for birdie. Nicklaus holed his four-footer for par leaving Jacklin with a short putt to tie Nicklaus. If he holed the putt it would be a tie but a miss by Jacklin would result in an outright win by the Americans.

Before Jacklin could putt, Nicklaus conceded the Englishman's putt thereby ensuring a tie. "I don't think you would have missed that Tony," Nicklaus reportedly said, "but under these circumstances I'd never give you the opportunity."

"The length of the putt has varied after thirty years," Jacklin has stated recently to reporters. "It's been as long as four feet. But my recollection is twenty inches. Of course, I could have missed it; there are no guarantees in golf, especially in the crucible of the Ryder Cup, but I believe I would have made it. But Jack saw the big picture, two months before I had become the first British player in 18 years to win the Open, so there was very much a pro-British fervour at the Ryder Cup in England that year. Jack saw that the putt on the last hole in 1969 meant a heck of a lot more to the Ryder Cup than who won or lost that particular match. It was a great moment."

RULE **3** | **STROKE PLAY**

3-1 WINNER

The competitor who plays the *stipulated round* or rounds in the fewest strokes is the winner.

See **incident** concerning Rule 3-2 on page 21

3-2 FAILURE TO HOLE OUT

If a competitor fails to hole out at any hole and does not correct his mistake before he plays a *stroke* from the next *teeing ground* or, in the case of the last hole of the round, before he leaves the *putting green*, **he shall be disqualified**.

3-3 DOUBT AS TO PROCEDURE
a Procedure

In stroke play only, when during play of a hole a competitor is doubtful of his rights or procedure, he may, without penalty, play a second ball. After the situation which caused the doubt has arisen, the competitor should, before taking further action, announce to his *marker* or a *fellow-competitor* his decision to invoke this Rule and the ball with which he will score if the *Rules* permit.

The competitor shall report the facts to the *Committee* before returning his score card unless he scores the same with both balls; if he fails to do so, **he shall be disqualified**.

b Determination of Score for Hole

If the *Rules* allow the procedure selected in advance by the competitor, the score with the ball selected shall be his score for the hole.

If the competitor fails to announce in advance his decision to invoke this Rule or his selection, the score with the original ball or, if the original ball is not one of the balls being played, the first ball put into play shall count if the *Rules* allow the procedure adopted for such ball.

Note 1: If a competitor plays a second ball, *penalty strokes* incurred solely by playing the ball ruled not to count and *strokes* subsequently taken with that ball shall be disregarded.

Note 2: A second ball played under Rule 3-3 is not a *provisional ball* under Rule 27-2.

3-4 REFUSAL TO COMPLY WITH A RULE

If a competitor refuses to comply with a *Rule* affecting the rights of another competitor, **he shall be disqualified**.

3-5 GENERAL PENALTY

The penalty for a breach of a *Rule* in stroke play is two strokes except when otherwise provided.

RULE 3 INCIDENT

In the 1997 Volvo PGA Championship at Wentworth, on the 13th hole, Nick Faldo chipped his ball from just off the green, the ball coming to rest against the flagstick. At this time the ball was not holed as all of the ball was not below the level of the lip of the hole.

21

While Faldo acknowledged the applause of the crowd and passed his club back to his caddie, his fellow-competitor, Ernie Els, walked to the hole, lifted Faldo's ball and returned it to him. The incident was televised and a number of viewers telephoned the Tournament Office concerned that Faldo's ball may not have been "holed" before Els picked it up.

The incident was reviewed by officials as Faldo completed his round and it transpired that, off camera, the ball had fallen into the hole before Els lifted it from the hole and therefore there was no question of Faldo having breached Rule 3-2 for failing to hole out.

CLUBS AND THE BALL

The Royal and Ancient Golf Club of St Andrews reserves the right to change the *Rules* and make and change the interpretations relating to clubs, balls and other implements at any time.

RULE ## CLUBS

A player in doubt as to the conformity of a club should consult the Royal and Ancient Golf Club of St Andrews.

A manufacturer should submit to the Royal and Ancient Golf Club of St Andrews a sample of a club which is to be manufactured for a ruling as to whether the club conforms with the *Rules*. If a manufacturer fails to submit a sample before manufacturing and/or marketing the club, the manufacturer assumes the risk of a ruling that the club does not conform with the Rules. Any sample submitted to the Royal and Ancient Golf Club of St Andrews will become its property for reference purposes.

4-1 FORM AND MAKE OF CLUBS
a General
The player's clubs shall conform with this Rule and the provisions, specifications and interpretations set forth in Appendix II.

b Wear and Alteration
A club which conforms with the *Rules* when new is deemed to conform after wear through normal use. Any part of a club which has been purposely altered is regarded as new and must, in its altered state, conform with the Rules.

4-2 PLAYING CHARACTERISTICS CHANGED AND FOREIGN MATERIAL
a Playing Characteristics Changed
During a *stipulated round,* the playing characteristics of a club shall not be purposely changed by adjustment or by any other means.

b Foreign Material

Foreign material must not be applied to the club face for the purpose of influencing the movement of the ball.

PENALTY FOR BREACH OF RULE 4-1 or -2:

Disqualification.

4-3 DAMAGED CLUBS: REPAIR AND REPLACEMENT

a Damage in Normal Course of Play

If, during a *stipulated round*, a player's club is damaged in the normal course of play, he may:

(i) use the club in its damaged state for the remainder of the *stipulated round*; or

(ii) without unduly delaying play, repair it or have it repaired; or

(iii) as an additional option available only if the club is unfit for play, replace the damaged club with any club. The replacement of a club must not unduly delay play and must not be made by borrowing any club selected for play by any other person playing on the *course*.

PENALTY FOR BREACH OF RULE 4-3a:

See Penalty Statement for Rule 4-4a or b.

Note: A club is unfit for play if it is substantially damaged, e.g. the shaft breaks into pieces or the clubhead becomes loose, detached or significantly deformed. A club is not unfit for play solely because the shaft is bent, the club's lie or loft has been altered or the clubhead is scratched.

b Damage Other Than in Normal Course of Play

If, during a *stipulated round*, a player's club is damaged other than in the normal course of play rendering it non-conforming or changing its playing characteristics, the club shall not subsequently be used or replaced during the round.

See **incident** involving Rule 4-3b on page 25

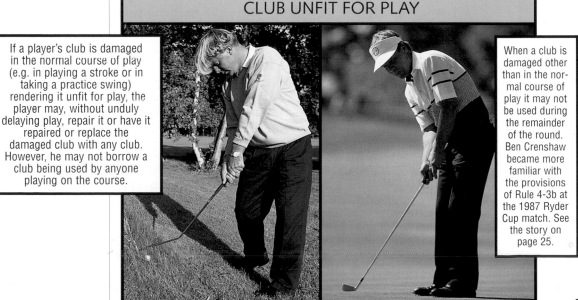

CLUB UNFIT FOR PLAY

If a player's club is damaged in the normal course of play (e.g. in playing a stroke or in taking a practice swing) rendering it unfit for play, the player may, without unduly delaying play, repair it or have it repaired or replace the damaged club with any club. However, he may not borrow a club being used by anyone playing on the course.

When a club is damaged other than in the normal course of play it may not be used during the remainder of the round. Ben Crenshaw became more familiar with the provisions of Rule 4-3b at the 1987 Ryder Cup match. See the story on page 25.

BREACH OF 14-CLUB RULE IN MATCH PLAY

I've just realised I have 15 clubs in my bag. I'll declare my 2-iron out of play, but what is the score in our match?

As I was already 2 up and the two hole penalty applies to the match score, I am now 4 up.

c Damage Prior to Round

A player may use a club damaged prior to a round provided the club, in its damaged state, conforms with the *Rules*.

Damage to a club which occurred prior to a round may be repaired during the round, provided the playing characteristics are not changed and play is not unduly delayed.

PENALTY FOR BREACH OF RULE 4-3b or c:

Disqualification.

(Undue delay – see Rule 6-7.)

4-4 MAXIMUM OF FOURTEEN CLUBS
a Selection and Addition of Clubs

The player shall start a *stipulated round* with not more than fourteen clubs. He is limited to the clubs thus selected for that round except that, if he started with fewer than fourteen clubs, he may add any number provided his total number does not exceed fourteen.

The addition of a club or clubs must not unduly delay play (Rule 6-7) and must not be made by borrowing any club selected for play by any other person playing on the course.

b Partners May Share Clubs

Partners may share clubs, provided that the total number of clubs carried by the partners so sharing does not exceed fourteen.

PENALTY FOR BREACH OF RULE 4-4a or b,

REGARDLESS OF NUMBER OF EXCESS CLUBS CARRIED:

Match play — At the conclusion of the hole at which the breach is discovered, the state of the match shall be adjusted by deducting one hole for each hole at which a breach occurred. Maximum deduction per round: two holes.

Stroke play — Two strokes for each hole at which any breach occurred; maximum penalty per round: four strokes.

Bogey and par competitions — Penalties as in match play.

Stableford competitions — see Note to Rule 32-1b.

c Excess Club Declared Out of Play

Any club carried or used in breach of this Rule shall be declared out of play by the player immediately upon discovery that a breach has occurred and thereafter shall not be used by the player during the round.

PENALTY FOR BREACH OF RULE 4-4c:

Disqualification.

RULE 4 INCIDENT

As Ben Crenshaw walked down a gravel pathway at Muirfield Village during the 1987 Ryder Cup, he was bouncing his putter along the ground in time with his steps when the club's shaft broke.

It was the third and final day of the competition and Crenshaw was competing against Eamonn Darcy in the singles. The American team had finished the previous day trailing the European team by five points. The matches in front of Crenshaw and Darcy were tilting in favour of the Americans, and those behind could go either way so every point had become crucial.

It did not matter that Crenshaw's putter was damaged without anger or malice. Because the club was damaged "other than in the normal course of play," America's best putter would now suffer the consequences of Rule 4. He could not use the putter, repair it or replace it.

For the remainder of the match Crenshaw used various clubs for putting – sometimes a 1-iron, sometimes a sand wedge. The Texan's misfortune, coupled with the intensity of the Ryder Cup singles competition, seemed to provide extraordinary focus and he continued to putt well, especially well since he didn't have a putter. The match went to the 18th hole where Darcy won 1 up.

With a final score of 15-13, the European team won the Ryder Cup for the first time on American soil.

RULE **5** | # THE BALL

5-1 GENERAL

The ball the player uses shall conform to requirements specified in Appendix III.

Note: The *Committee* may require, in the conditions of a competition (Rule 33-1), that the ball the player uses must be named on the current List of Conforming Golf Balls issued by the Royal and Ancient Golf Club of St Andrews.

5-2 FOREIGN MATERIAL

Foreign material must not be applied to a ball for the purpose of changing its playing characteristics.

PENALTY FOR BREACH OF RULE 5-1 or -2:

Disqualification.

See **incident** involving Rule 5-3 on page 28

5-3 BALL UNFIT FOR PLAY

A ball is unfit for play if it is visibly cut, cracked or out of shape. A ball is not unfit for play solely because mud or other materials adhere to it, its surface is scratched or scraped or its paint is damaged or discoloured.

If a player has reason to believe his ball has become unfit for play during the play of the hole being played, he may during the play of such hole lift his ball without penalty to determine whether it is unfit.

Before lifting the ball, the player must announce his intention to his opponent in match play or his *marker* or a *fellow-competitor* in stroke play and mark the position of the ball. He may then lift and examine the ball without cleaning it and must give his opponent, marker or fellow-competitor an opportunity to examine the ball.

If he fails to comply with this procedure, **he shall incur a penalty of one stroke**.

If it is determined that the ball has become unfit for play during play of the hole being played, the player may substitute another ball, placing it on the spot where the original ball lay. Otherwise, the original ball shall be replaced.

If a ball breaks into pieces as a result of a *stroke*, the stroke shall be cancelled and the player shall play a ball without penalty as nearly as possible at the spot from which the original ball was played (see Rule 20-5).

*PENALTY FOR BREACH OF RULE 5-3:
Match play — Loss of hole; Stroke play — Two strokes.
If a player incurs the general penalty for breach of Rule 5-3, no additional penalty under the Rule shall be applied.

Note: If the opponent, marker or fellow-competitor wishes to dispute a claim of unfitness, he must do so before the player plays another ball. (Cleaning ball lifted from putting green or under any other Rule — see Rule 21.)

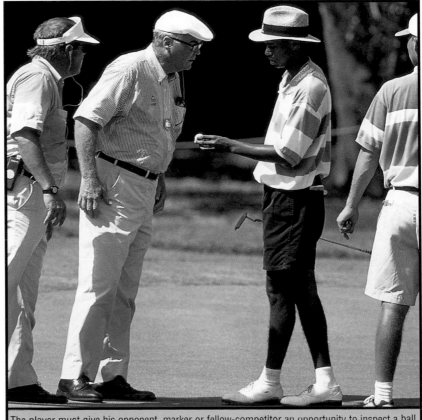

The player must give his opponent, marker or fellow-competitor an opportunity to inspect a ball that a player believes is unfit for play. In some cases, a referee may be asked to participate in this process. See the story on page 28 involving Tiger Woods at the 1994 U.S. Amateur.

RULE 5 INCIDENT

On the 32nd hole of the final of the 1994 U.S. Amateur Championship, Tiger Woods learned that one of the very specific instances in the Rules when a referee is not to be involved, except as a last resort, is in determining whether or not a ball is unfit for play during the play of a hole.

One down to Trip Kuehne with five holes left in the 36-hole match, Woods' drive from the 14th tee of the TPC at Sawgrass struck a cart path and a media vehicle before finally coming to rest.

Having played his second shot on to the putting green, Woods marked and lifted his ball. It was then that he questioned whether or not his ball had been rendered unfit for play by virtue of its striking the path and the vehicle. Woods' inquiry was directed to the referee who was walking with the match. The referee responded that Woods would have to make that determination after giving his opponent an opportunity to examine the ball.

After inspecting Woods' ball, Kuehne said he was unsure whether or not it was unfit. This sent Woods back to the referee for an opinion.

While Decision 5-3/7 permits a referee to make such a decision, it also states that every effort should be made to have the opponent, marker or fellow-competitor fulfill his responsibilities under Rule 5-3. In this situation, Woods' opponent was not able to fulfill his responsibilities because he did not know if a ball was unfit simply because it was scarred from bouncing off of a cart path.

With Kuehne unsure and Woods entitled to a ruling, the referee determined that a new ball could not be substituted. Rule 5-3 is specific in stating that a ball is not unfit when its surface is scratched or scraped or its paint is damaged or discoloured.

Woods halved the hole with the scraped ball. After birdies at the 16th and 17th, Woods was 1 up. Woods' par, at the 18th, gave him a 2 up victory and the first of his three consecutive U.S. Amateur titles.

RULE | # THE PLAYER

DEFINITION

A **marker** is one who is appointed by the *Committee* to record a *competitor's* score in stroke play. He may be a *fellow-competitor*. He is not a *referee*.

6-1 RULES; CONDITIONS OF COMPETITION
The player is responsible for knowing the *Rules* and the conditions under which the competition is to be played (Rule 33-1).

6-2 HANDICAP
a Match Play
Before starting a match in a handicap competition, the players should determine from one another their respective handicaps. If a player begins

the match having declared a higher handicap which would affect the number of strokes given or received, **he shall be disqualified**; otherwise, the player shall play off the declared handicap.

b Stroke Play

In any round of a handicap competition, the competitor shall ensure that his handicap is recorded on his score card before it is returned to the *Committee*. If no handicap is recorded on his score card before it is returned, or if the recorded handicap is higher than that to which he is entitled and this affects the number of strokes received, **he shall be disqualified** from the handicap competition; otherwise, the score shall stand.

Note: It is the player's responsibility to know the holes at which handicap strokes are to be given or received.

6-3 TIME OF STARTING AND GROUPS
a Time of Starting

The player shall start at the time laid down by the *Committee*.

b Groups

In stroke play, the competitor shall remain throughout the round in the group arranged by the *Committee* unless the Committee authorises or ratifies a change.

PENALTY FOR BREACH OF RULE 6-3:

Disqualification.

(Best-ball and four-ball play — see Rules 30-3a and 31-2.)

Note: The *Committee* may provide in the conditions of a competition (Rule 33-1) that, if the player arrives at his starting point, ready to play, within five minutes after his starting time, in the absence of circumstances which warrant waiving the penalty of disqualification as provided in Rule 33-7, the penalty for failure to start on time is **loss of the first hole in match play or two strokes at the first hole in stroke play** instead of disqualification.

6-4 CADDIE

The player may have only one *caddie* at any one time, **under penalty of disqualification**.

For any breach of a *Rule* by his caddie, the player incurs the applicable penalty.

6-5 BALL

The responsibility for playing the proper ball rests with the player. Each player should put an identification mark on his ball.

6-6 SCORING IN STROKE PLAY
a Recording Scores

After each hole the *marker* should check the score with the competitor and record it. On completion of the round the marker shall sign the card and hand it to the competitor. If more than one marker records the scores, each shall sign for the part for which he is responsible.

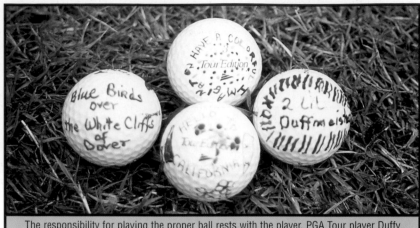

The responsibility for playing the proper ball rests with the player. PGA Tour player Duffy Waldorf has his wife and children assist him in putting identification marks on his golf balls.

See **incident** involving Rule 6-6b on page 35

b Signing and Returning Card

After completion of the round, the competitor should check his score for each hole and settle any doubtful points with the *Committee*. He shall ensure that the marker has signed the card, countersign the card himself and return it to the Committee as soon as possible.

PENALTY FOR BREACH OF RULE 6-6b:

Disqualification.

c Alteration of Card

No alteration may be made on a card after the competitor has returned it to the *Committee*.

See **incident** involving Rule 6-6d on page 34

d Wrong Score for Hole

The competitor is responsible for the correctness of the score recorded for each hole on his card. If he returns a score for any hole lower than actually taken, **he shall be disqualified**. If he returns a score for any hole higher

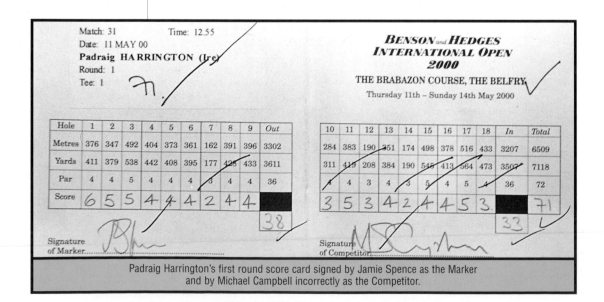

Padraig Harrington's first round score card signed by Jamie Spence as the Marker and by Michael Campbell incorrectly as the Competitor.

SCORING IN STROKE PLAY

COMPETITION __SPRING STROKE PLAY__   DATE __14 . 6 . 2000__

PLAYER __D. BROWN__   HANDICAP __10__   Game No __21__

Hole	Yards	Par	Stroke Index	Score	W = + L = - H = 0 POINTS	Mar Score	Hole	Yards	Par	Stroke Index	Score	W = + L = - H = 0 POINTS	Mar Score
1	312	4	17	5		6	10	369	4	12	6 5 (c)		
2	446	4	1	4		4	11	433	4	2	3		
3	310	4	13	4		3	12	361	4	14	4		
4	370	4	9	5	(b)	5	13	415	4	6	5		
5	478	5	3	6			14	155	3	16	6		
8 7	429	4	11	4			15	338	4	8	5		
7 6	385	4	5	3			16	316	4	10	4		
8	178	3	7	4			17	191	3	4	5		
9	354	4	15	6			18	508	5	18	7		
OUT	3262			41			IN	3086	35		44		
							OUT	3262	36		41		
							TOTAL	6348	71		85		

(a)

Markers Signature __D. B.__ (e & f)

HANDICAP __10__ (d)
NETT __75__

Players Signature __Bill White__

Competitor's Responsibilities:

1. To record the correct handicap somewhere on the score card before it is returned to the Committee.
2. To check the gross score recorded for each hole is correct.
3. To ensure that the marker has signed the card and to countersign the card himself before it is returned to the Committee.

Committee Responsibilities:

1. Issue to each competitor a score card containing the date and the competitor's name.
2. To add the scores for each hole and apply the handicap recorded on the card.

(**a**) Hole numbers may be altered if hole scores have been recorded in the wrong boxes.
(**b**) A marker need not keep a record of his own score, however it is recommended.
(**c**) There is nothing in the Rules that requires an alteration to be initialled.
(**d**) The competitor is responsible only for the correctness of the score recorded for each hole. If the competitor records a wrong total score or net score, the Committee must correct the error, without penalty to the competitor. In this instance, the Committee have added the scores for each hole and applied the handicap.
(**e**) There is no penalty if a marker signs the competitor's score card in the space provided for the competitor's signature, and the competitor then signs in the space provided for the marker's signature.
(**f**) The initialing of the score card by the competitor is sufficient for the purpose of countersignature.

than actually taken, the score as returned shall stand.

Note 1: The *Committee* is responsible for the addition of scores and application of the handicap recorded on the card — see Rule 33-5.

Note 2: In four-ball stroke play, see also Rule 31-4 and -7a.

6-7 UNDUE DELAY; SLOW PLAY

The player shall play without undue delay and in accordance with any pace of play guidelines which may be laid down by the *Committee*. Between completion of a hole and playing from the next *teeing ground*, the player shall not unduly delay play.

PENALTY FOR BREACH OF RULE 6-7:

Match play — Loss of hole; Stroke play — Two strokes.

Bogey and par competitions — See Note 2 to Rule 32-1a.

Stableford competitions — See Note 2 to Rule 32-1b.

For subsequent offence — Disqualification.

Note 1: If the player unduly delays play between holes, he is delaying the play of the next hole and, except for bogey, par and stableford competitions (see Rule 32), the penalty applies to that hole.

Note 2: For the purpose of preventing slow play, the *Committee* may, in the conditions of a competition (Rule 33-1), lay down pace of play guidelines including maximum periods of time allowed to complete a stipulated round, a hole or a stroke.

In stroke play only, the Committee may, in such a condition, modify the penalty for a breach of this Rule as follows:

First offence — One stroke;

Second offence — Two strokes.

For subsequent offence — Disqualification.

UNDUE DELAY: ENTERING CLUBHOUSE

6-8 DISCONTINUANCE OF PLAY; RESUMPTION OF PLAY
a When Permitted

The player shall not discontinue play unless:

(i)   the *Committee* has suspended play;

(ii) he believes there is danger from lightning;

(iii) he is seeking a decision from the *Committee* on a doubtful or disputed point (see Rules 2-5 and 34-3); or

(iv) there is some other good reason such as sudden illness.

Bad weather is not of itself a good reason for discontinuing play.

 If the player discontinues play without specific permission from the *Committee*, he shall report to the Committee as soon as practicable. If he does so and the Committee considers his reason satisfactory, the player incurs no penalty. Otherwise, **the player shall be disqualified**.

Exception in match play: Players discontinuing match play by agreement are not subject to disqualification unless by so doing the competition is delayed.

Note: Leaving the course does not of itself constitute discontinuance of play.

b Procedure When Play Suspended by Committee

When play is suspended by the *Committee*, if the players in a match or group are between the play of two holes, they shall not resume play until the Committee has ordered a resumption of play. If they are in the process of playing a hole, they may continue provided they do so without delay. If they choose to continue, they shall discontinue either before or immediately after completing the hole.

The players shall resume play when the Committee has ordered a resumption of play.

PENALTY FOR BREACH OF RULE 6-8b:

Disqualification.

Note: The *Committee* may provide in the conditions of a competition (Rule 33-1) that, in potentially dangerous situations, play shall be discontinued immediately following a suspension of play by the Committee. If a player fails to discontinue play immediately, **he shall be disqualified** unless circumstances warrant waiving such penalty as provided in Rule 33-7.

c Lifting Ball When Play Discontinued

When a player discontinues play of a hole under Rule 6-8a, he may lift his ball without penalty only if the *Committee* has suspended play or there is a good reason to lift it. Before lifting the ball the player must mark its position. If the player discontinues play and lifts his ball without specific permission from the Committee, when reporting to the Committee (Rule 6-8a), he shall, at that time, report the lifting of the ball.

If the player lifts the ball without a good reason to do so, fails to mark the position of the ball before lifting it or fails to report the lifting of the ball, **he shall incur a penalty of one stroke**.

d Procedure When Play Resumed

Play shall be resumed from where it was discontinued, even if resumption occurs on a subsequent day. The player shall, either before or when play is resumed, proceed as follows:

(i) if the player has lifted the ball, he shall, provided he was entitled to lift it under Rule 6-8c, place a ball on the spot from which the original ball was lifted. Otherwise, the original ball must be replaced;

(ii) if the player entitled to lift his ball under Rule 6-8c has not done so, he may lift, clean and replace the ball, or substitute a ball on the spot from which the original ball was lifted. Before lifting the ball he must mark its position; or

(iii) if the player's ball or ball-marker is moved (including by wind or water) while play is discontinued, a ball or ball-marker shall be placed on the spot from which the original ball or ball-marker was moved.

(Spot not determinable — see Rule 20-3c.)

*PENALTY FOR BREACH OF RULE 6-8d:

Match play — Loss of hole; Stroke play — Two strokes.

*If a player incurs the general penalty for a breach of Rule 6–8d, no additional penalty under Rule 6-8c shall be applied.

RULE 6 INCIDENTS

As the ultimate testament to a player's performance on the course in a stroke play competition, the score card must never contain a score lower than actually taken and it must be signed by the competitor, attested by

A solemn Padraig Harrington following his final day disqualification from the 2000 Benson & Hedges International for failing to sign his first round score card.

the marker and returned as soon as possible to the Committee. Failure to meet any of these criteria results in disqualification.

Roberto De Vicenzo signed for a higher score than he actually made at the 1968 Masters Tournament, which did not disqualify him but it kept the Argentinean from forcing a play-off with Bob Goalby.

Playing in front of Goalby on Sunday, De Vicenzo, the reigning Open Champion, sank a five-foot birdie putt on the 17th hole for a 3. A bogey at the 18th gave him an 11-under total of 277. Goalby managed a five-footer for par at the 18th for a 66 and another 277.

However, De Vicenzo's fellow-competitor and marker, Tommy Aaron, had mistakenly given De Vicenzo a 4 at the 17th rather than the 3. De Vicenzo had not noticed the mistake, signed and returned the score card, and rushed away from the scorer's table for press interviews. A little later, Aaron noticed the mistake and brought it to the attention of tournament officials.

Augusta National founder Bob Jones searched for a way around the ensuing ruling but none could be found. Once the score card was signed and returned, the decision under the Rules was straightforward: the higher score must stand. Goalby was the Masters Champion.

An hour later, De Vicenzo told the media, "It's my fault. Tommy feels like I feel, very bad. I think the Rule is hard." The day's drama was compounded by the fact that it was De Vincenzo's 45th birthday.

Failure to sign his first round score card arguably cost Padraig Harrington the 2000 Benson and Hedges International Open at The Belfry. As he began warming up for the final round, holding a five-shot lead, the 28-year-old Irishman was informed by officials of a problem.

Members of the Committee had begun to collect Harrington's three previous score cards for souvenir purposes when it was noticed that he had not signed his first round card. Jamie Spence, his marker, had signed the card as required, but Michael Campbell, the other player in the group had mistakenly signed instead of Harrington. The resulting penalty under Rule 6-6b was disqualification.

RULE

PRACTICE

DEFINITION

The **course** is the whole area within which play is permitted (see Rule 33-2).

See **incident** involving Rule 7-1 on page 37

7-1 BEFORE OR BETWEEN ROUNDS
a Match Play
On any day of a match play competition, a player may practice on the competition *course* before a round.

b Stroke Play
On any day of a stroke competition or play-off, a competitor shall not practice on the competition *course* or test the surface of any *putting green* on the course before a round or play-off. When two or more rounds of a stroke competition are to be played over consecutive days, a competitor shall not practice between those rounds on any competition course remaining to be played, or test the surface of any putting green on such course.
Exception: Practice putting or chipping on or near the first *teeing ground* before starting a round or play-off is permitted.

PENALTY FOR BREACH OF RULE 7-1b:

Disqualification.

Note: The *Committee* may in the conditions of a competition (Rule 33-1) prohibit practice on the competition course on any day of a match play competition or permit practice on the competition course or part of the course (Rule 33-2c) on any day of or between rounds of a stroke competition.

See **incident** involving Rule 7-2 on page 37

7-2 DURING ROUND
A player shall not play a practice *stroke* either during the play of a hole or between the play of two holes except that, between the play of two holes, the player may practice putting or chipping on or near the *putting green* of the hole last played, any practice putting green or the *teeing ground* of the next hole to be played in the round, provided such practice stroke is not played from a hazard and does not unduly delay play (Rule 6-7).

Strokes played in continuing the play of a hole, the result of which has been decided, are not practice strokes.
Exception: When play has been suspended by the *Committee*, a player may, prior to resumption of play, practise (a) as provided in this Rule, (b) anywhere other than on the competition *course* and (c) as otherwise permitted by the Committee.

PENALTY FOR BREACH OF RULE 7-2:

Match play — Loss of hole; Stroke play — Two strokes.

PRACTICE DURING A ROUND

Practice putting and chipping on or near the tee of the next hole to be played is permitted as long as play is not delayed.

In the event of a breach between the play of two holes, the penalty applies to the next hole.

Note 1: A practice swing is not a practice *stroke* and may be taken at any place, provided the player does not breach the *Rules*.

Note 2: The *Committee* may prohibit practice on or near the *putting green* of the hole last played.

RULE 7 INCIDENTS

The former Masters and Open Champion, Sandy Lyle, was disqualified from the 2000 Hope Chrysler Classic for practising between rounds during the Tournament.

After play had been completed in the third round, a member of the greenstaff was surprised to see Lyle practising on the 18th green and mentioned it to a member of the Tournament Committee. When officials asked Lyle about his actions and the player confirmed that he had returned to the 18th green to practice his putting, the Committee had no option but to disqualify him for a breach of Rule 7-1b.

After a suspension of play during the fourth round of the 2001 Players Championship at Sawgrass, both the penultimate group and the final group were required to resume play from the 10th tee. Tiger Woods, playing in the final group, was aware that the group in front would resume play first and that he would have additional time to arrive at the 10th tee.

Officials, concerned that Woods may have continued to hit practice shots on the practice range after the signal for a resumption of play had been sounded, advised Woods that such action would be in breach of Rule 7-2. Play was resumed without incident and Woods went on to win The Players Championship by one stroke from Vijay Singh.

RULE ADVICE; INDICATING LINE OF PLAY

DEFINITIONS

Advice is any counsel or suggestion which could influence a player in determining his play, the choice of a club or the method of making a *stroke*.
 Information on the *Rules* or on matters of public information, such as the position of *hazards* or the *flagstick* on the *putting green*, is not advice.
 The **line of play** is the direction which the player wishes his ball to take after a *stroke*, plus a reasonable distance on either side of the intended direction. The line of play extends vertically upwards from the ground, but does not extend beyond the *hole*.

See **incident** involving Rule 8-1 on page 39

8-1 ADVICE

During a *stipulated round*, a player shall not give *advice* to anyone in the competition except his partner and may ask for advice only from his partner or either of their caddies.

8-2 INDICATING LINE OF PLAY
a Other Than on Putting Green

Except on the *putting green*, a player may have the *line of play* indicated to him by anyone, but no one shall be positioned by the player on or close to the line or an extension of the line beyond the hole while the *stroke* is being played. Any mark placed during the play of a hole by the player or with his knowledge to indicate the line shall be removed before the stroke is played.

Exception: Flagstick attended or held up — see Rule 17-1.

ADVICE

38

INDICATING LINE OF PLAY

No. I am afraid you may not.

I think I will putt this. May I place a mark at the top of the rise to indicate a line?

See **incident** involving Rule 8-2b below

b On the Putting Green

When the player's ball is on the *putting green*, the player, his partner or either of their caddies may, before but not during the *stroke*, point out a line for putting, but in so doing the putting green shall not be touched. No mark shall be placed anywhere to indicate a line for putting.

PENALTY FOR BREACH OF RULE:

Match play — Loss of hole; Stroke play — Two strokes.

Note: The *Committee* may, in the conditions of a team competition (Rule 33-1), permit each team to appoint one person who may give *advice* (including pointing out a line for putting) to members of that team. The Committee may lay down conditions relating to the appointment and permitted conduct of such person, who must be identified to the Committee before giving advice.

RULE 8 INCIDENTS

During the third round of the 1991 PGA Championship while advising John Daly about the break of a putt on Crooked Stick's 11th green, Daly's caddie, Jeff "Squeeky" Medlen, accidentally touched the green with the flagstick.

As ninth alternate, Daly had been included in the championship field when Nick Price withdrew to be present at the birth of his child, and three alternates ahead of Daly declined for various reasons. The unknown Arkansan had taken the outright lead for the title after posting a 69 and 67 for the first and second rounds respectively. Playing with Bruce Lietzke on Saturday, Daly was on his way to a third round 69. At the 11th, Medlen used his hand to point out the line of Daly's first putt. In his other hand, Medlen held the flagstick and inadvertently allowed it to touch the green.

The potential breach of the rules was televised to millions and, fortunately, videotaped for review. Alerted almost immediately to what had taken place, Rules officials met Daly at the end of the round to discuss the matter and make a decision before Daly returned his score card.

Daly, Medlen, Lietzke and Rules officials reviewed the videotape. The tape showed Medlen holding the removed flagstick and allowing it to touch the putting green about three feet to the right of the hole while indicating the line of putt with his other hand. Rule 8-2 states that, while a line for putting may be pointed out, the green shall not be touched in doing so.

After speaking with all involved and watching the tape, officials were satisfied that no penalty was incurred. Daly returned his third round card with a score of 69. The following day, he won the PGA Championship by three shots.

That part of Rule 8 relating to giving or asking for advice states, in part, that a player must not give advice to anyone in the competition except his partner. In the final round of the 1980 Tournament of Champions Tom Watson was playing with Lee Trevino. Having played together so often over the years, Watson knew Trevino's swing well and noticed a little flaw in it that day. He casually told Trevino about it. The television commentator at the time noted it as a friendly gesture between two tournament players, but viewers called in to point out that such assistance constituted giving advice, contrary to Rule 8-1.

After the round, Watson was asked whether he had given Trevino some guidance on his swing and a reply in the affirmative resulted in Watson incurring a two stroke penalty under the advice Rule. Fortunately, Watson had a three stroke lead at the conclusion of the 72 holes and the imposition of the two stroke penalty did not, therefore, prevent him from winning the Tournament.

RULE **INFORMATION AS TO STROKES TAKEN**

9-1 GENERAL

The number of *strokes* a player has taken shall include any penalty strokes incurred.

9-2 MATCH PLAY

See **incident** involving Rule 9-2 on page 41

A player who has incurred a penalty shall inform his opponent as soon as practicable, unless he is obviously proceeding under a *Rule* involving a penalty and this has been observed by his opponent. If he fails so to inform his opponent, he shall be deemed to have given wrong information, even if he was not aware that he had incurred a penalty.

An opponent is entitled to ascertain from the player, during the play of a hole, the number of strokes he has taken and, after play of a hole, the number of strokes taken on the hole just completed.

If during the play of a hole the player gives or is deemed to give wrong information as to the number of strokes taken, he shall incur no penalty if he corrects the mistake before his opponent has played his next stroke. If the player fails so to correct the wrong information, **he shall lose the hole**.

If after play of a hole the player gives or is deemed to give wrong information as to the number of strokes taken on the hole just completed and this affects the opponent's understanding of the result of the hole, he shall incur no penalty if he corrects his mistake before any player plays from the next *teeing ground* or, in the case of the last hole of the match, before all players leave the *putting green*. If the player fails so to correct the wrong information, **he shall lose the hole**.

9-3 STROKE PLAY

A competitor who has incurred a penalty should inform his *marker* as soon as practicable.

RULE 9 INCIDENT

On the 7th tee of Kiawah Island's Ocean Course during the first morning's foursomes of the 1991 Ryder Cup Matches, Chip Beck and Paul Azinger were overheard by their European opponents discussing which type of ball they would use to optimise their performance during the play of that hole.

The Americans mistakenly believed that because one of them played a 90-compression ball and the other a 100-compression ball, they were entitled to a choice as to which they could use.

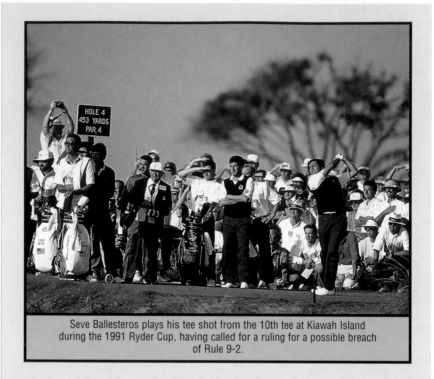

Seve Ballesteros plays his tee shot from the 10th tee at Kiawah Island during the 1991 Ryder Cup, having called for a ruling for a possible breach of Rule 9-2.

A variation of the "One-Ball Condition" was in effect which allowed both players to play their preferred brand and type of ball when it was their turn to play from the tee. However, once that determination was made on the first two holes, each player was limited to using that brand and type of ball thereafter.

Unknowingly and mistakenly, the Americans made the choice and the wrong type of ball was played from the tee. The European side of Seve Ballesteros and Jose Maria Olazabal suspected this was a breach of the Rules. Sam Torrance, a European team member who was not playing in the first morning's matches, was in the gallery and following the match. He was motioned over by Ballesteros, told of the situation and sent to fetch the European Captain Bernard Gallacher.

While Gallacher was being located, play of the 7th, 8th and 9th holes was completed. On the way to the 10th tee, the Europeans made a claim concerning what had taken place at the 7th hole. The chief referee was called to settle the dispute.

In match play, Rule 9-2 requires a player who has incurred a penalty to notify his opponent as soon as practicable. If he does not, even when he doesn't know he has incurred a penalty, he is considered to have given wrong information. In this case, the American side gave wrong information as a penalty was associated with their playing of the wrong type of ball from the 7th tee. However, since the European side was aware of the error and did not make a claim (Rule 2-5) before anyone played from the 8th tee, their belated claim could not be considered.

The match continued from the 10th tee without Beck and Azinger being penalised for their breach at the 7th hole.

RULE 10

DEFINITION

ORDER OF PLAY

The player who is to play first from the *teeing ground* is said to have the **honour**.

10-1 MATCH PLAY
a Teeing Ground
The side which shall have the *honour* at the first *teeing ground* shall be determined by the order of the draw. In the absence of a draw, the honour should be decided by lot.

The side which wins a hole shall take the honour at the next teeing ground. If a hole has been halved, the side which had the honour at the previous teeing ground shall retain it.

See **incident** involving Rule 10-1b on page 44

b Other Than on Teeing Ground
When the balls are *in play*, the ball farther from the hole shall be played first. If the balls are equidistant from the hole, the ball to be played first should be decided by lot.
Exception: Rule 30-3c (best-ball and four-ball match play).

c Playing Out of Turn
If a player plays when his opponent should have played, the opponent may immediately require the player to cancel the stroke so played and, in correct order, play a ball without penalty as nearly as possible at the spot from which the original ball was last played (see Rule 20-5).

10-2 STROKE PLAY
a Teeing Ground
The competitor who shall have the *honour* at the first *teeing ground* shall be determined by the order of the draw. In the absence of a draw, the honour should be decided by lot.

The competitor with the lowest score at a hole shall take the honour at the next teeing ground. The competitor with the second lowest score shall play next and so on. If two or more competitors have the same score at a hole, they shall play from the next teeing ground in the same order as at the previous teeing ground.

b Other Than on Teeing Ground
When the balls are *in play*, the ball farthest from the hole shall be played first. If two or more balls are equidistant from the hole, the ball to be played first should be decided by lot.
Exceptions: Rules 22 (ball interfering with or assisting play) and 31-5 (four-ball stroke play).

c Playing Out of Turn
If a competitor plays out of turn, no penalty is incurred and the ball shall be played as it lies. If, however, the *Committee* determines that competitors have agreed to play in an order other than that set forth in Clauses 2a, 2b and 3 of this Rule to give one of them an advantage, **they shall be disqualified.**

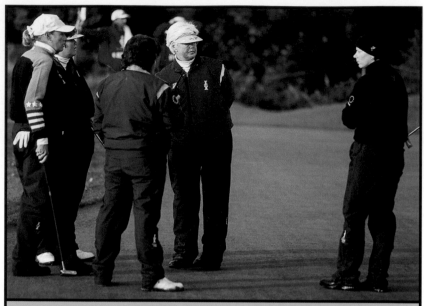

USA Captain, Pat Bradley, discusses with the Pat Hurst and Kelly Robbins their options before requiring Annika Sorenstam, who had played out of turn, to replay her chip shot at the 13th hole during the 2000 Solheim Cup.

(Playing stroke while another ball in motion after stroke from putting green — see Rule 16-1f.)

(Incorrect order of play in threesomes and foursomes stroke play — see Rule 29-3.)

10-3 PROVISIONAL BALL OR SECOND BALL FROM TEEING GROUND

If a player plays a *provisional ball* or a second ball from a *teeing ground*, he shall do so after his opponent or *fellow-competitor* has played his first *stroke*. If a player plays a provisional ball or a second ball out of turn, Clauses 1c and 2c of this Rule shall apply.

10-4 BALL MOVED IN MEASURING

If a ball is moved in measuring to determine which ball is farther from the hole, no penalty is incurred and the ball shall be replaced.

RULE 10 INCIDENT

After a suspension of play due to the course being in an unplayable condition during the 2000 Solheim Cup at Loch Lomond, Annika Sorenstam and Janice Moodie of the European Team returned to the 13th hole to resume their four-ball match against Kelly Robbins and Pat Hurst of the USA.

All four players were required to replace their balls in the spots from which they were lifted, as required by Rule 6-8d. Hurst was first to play from the fairway, with the other three balls either on or close to the putting green. Sorenstam played next, holing her chip from just off the green for a birdie 4.

Robbins, who had been talking to Hurst, walked back to where her ball marker lay to replace her ball on the putting green, then realised that it had been her turn to play and that Sorenstam had played out of turn. Rule 10-2b provides that the ball farther from the hole shall be played first and, in match play, if a player plays when her opponent should have played the opponent may require the player to cancel and replay the stroke in the correct order.

As Sorenstam had holed her chip shot it was clearly advantageous for the Americans to have the stroke cancelled and replayed. However, uncertain of whether to exercise their right they consulted with non-playing captain, Pat Bradley. After this consultation the Referee was advised that Sorenstam would be required to replay the stroke, which she failed to hole a second time. The hole was won by the Americans, with Pat Hurst making a birdie, and they went on to win the match by 2&1.

RULE 11 TEEING GROUND

DEFINITION

The **teeing ground** is the starting place for the hole to be played. It is a rectangular area two club-lengths in depth, the front and the sides of which are defined by the outside limits of two tee-markers. A ball is outside the teeing ground when all of it lies outside the teeing ground.

11-1 TEEING

In teeing, the ball may be placed on the ground, on an irregularity of surface created by the player on the ground or on a tee, sand or other substance in order to raise it off the ground.

A player may stand outside the *teeing ground* to play a ball within it.

11-2 TEE-MARKERS

Before a player plays his first *stroke* with any ball from the *teeing ground* of the hole being played, the tee-markers are deemed to be fixed. In such circumstances, if the player moves or allows to be moved a tee-marker for the purpose of avoiding interference with his stance, the area of his intended swing or his line of play, **he shall incur the penalty for a breach of Rule 13-2.**

11-3 BALL FALLING OFF TEE

If a ball, when not *in play*, falls off a tee or is knocked off a tee by the player in addressing it, it may be re-teed without penalty, but if a *stroke* is made at the ball in these circumstances, whether the ball is moving or not, the stroke counts but no penalty is incurred.

11-4 PLAYING FROM OUTSIDE TEEING GROUND
a Match Play

If a player, when starting a hole, plays a ball from outside the *teeing*

PLAYING FROM WRONG TEE IN STROKE PLAY

This doesn't look like the 7th hole. I think we are playing the wrong hole. What do we do now?

Unfortunately, we are both penalised two strokes and we must try and find the 7th tee to continue our round. Our drives on this hole do not count.

13th Tee

6th Green

7th Tee

ground, the opponent may immediately require the player to cancel the *stroke* so played and play a ball from within the teeing ground, without penalty.

See **incident** involving Rule 11-4b on page 47

b Stroke Play

If a competitor, when starting a hole, plays a ball from outside the *teeing ground*, **he shall incur a penalty of two strokes** and shall then play a ball from within the teeing ground.

If the competitor plays a stroke from the next teeing ground without first correcting his mistake or, in the case of the last hole of the round, leaves the *putting green* without first declaring his intention to correct his mistake, **he shall be disqualified**.

The stroke from outside the teeing ground and any subsequent strokes by the competitor on the hole prior to his correction of the mistake do not count in his score.

11-5 PLAYING FROM WRONG TEEING GROUND

The provisions of Rule 11-4 apply.

Mike Donald congratulates Hale Irwin after the 19th hole of the play-off for the 1990 US Open Championship – see incident below.

RULE 11 INCIDENT

At the 1990 US Open Championship the drama and competitive tension at Medinah Country Club had been intense all week. Hale Irwin had summoned a wave of talent reflective of his 33 professional victories, which included two previous U.S. Open victories in 1974 and 1979. Indeed, he had holed a 45-foot birdie putt on the 72nd hole of play to force 18 hole play-off with Mike Donald whose only PGA Tour victory had come the previous year in Williamsburg, Virginia.

The players walked off the 17th green of the play-off round with Donald leading by one. On the 18th tee Mike Donald teed up in front of the markers. The walking Referee noticed whereupon Donald was asked to re-tee the ball.

Rule 11, as it applies to stroke play, is exact. If a competitor plays from outside the teeing ground, he shall incur a penalty of two strokes and shall then play a ball from within the teeing ground. Had Donald's mistake been observed a few moments later, after he had played from ahead of the markers, the resulting two-stroke penalty would have reversed that state of the play-off and given Irwin a one-stroke lead.

The Referee's intervention prevented the breach, but Donald's bogey at the 90th hole resulted in both men scoring 74 in the play-off round. By the terms and conditions outlined in the entry form, and for the first time in its history, the U.S. Open then moved to sudden death to determine the winner.

On the first sudden death hole, the 91st hole of the championship, Irwin holed a eight-foot birdie putt to become the U.S. Open's oldest winner.

RULE **12** | SEARCHING FOR AND IDENTIFYING BALL

DEFINITIONS

A **hazard** is any *bunker* or *water hazard*.

A **bunker** is a *hazard* consisting of a prepared area of ground, often a hollow, from which turf or soil has been removed and replaced with sand or the like. Grass-covered ground bordering or within a bunker is not part of the bunker. The margin of a bunker extends vertically downwards, but not upwards. A ball is in a bunker when it lies in or any part of it touches the bunker.

A **water hazard** is any sea, lake, pond, river, ditch, surface drainage ditch or other open water course (whether or not containing water) and anything of a similar nature.

All ground or water within the margin of a water hazard is part of the water hazard. The margin of a water hazard extends vertically upwards and downwards. Stakes and lines defining the margins of water hazards are in the hazards. Such stakes are *obstructions*. A ball is in a water hazard when it lies in or any part of it touches the water hazard.

Note 1: Water hazards (other than *lateral water hazards*) should be defined by yellow stakes or lines.

Note 2: The *Committee* may make a Local Rule prohibiting play from an environmentally-sensitive area which has been defined as a water hazard.

12-1 SEARCHING FOR BALL; SEEING BALL

See **incident** involving Rule 12-1 on page 50

In searching for his ball anywhere on the *course*, the player may touch or bend long grass, rushes, bushes, whins, heather or the like, but only to the extent necessary to find and identify it, provided that this does not improve the lie of the ball, the area of his intended swing or his *line of play*.

SEARCHING FOR BALL IN BUNKER

If a player's ball is buried in a bunker, he may search for it by probing the sand with his fingers or he may use a rake. If the ball is moved, there is no penalty, but it must be replaced and, if necessary, re-covered so that only part of it is visible.

A player is not necessarily entitled to see his ball when playing a *stroke*.

In a *hazard*, if a ball is believed to be covered by *loose impediments* or sand, the player may remove by probing, raking or other means as much thereof as will enable him to see a part of the ball. If an excess is removed, no penalty is incurred and the ball shall be re-covered so that only a part of the ball is visible. If the ball is moved in such removal, no penalty is incurred; the ball shall be replaced and, if necessary, re-covered. As to removal of loose impediments outside a hazard, see Rule 23.

If a ball lying in an *abnormal ground condition* is accidentally moved during search, no penalty is incurred; the ball shall be replaced, unless the player elects to proceed under Rule 25-1b. If the player replaces the ball, he may still proceed under Rule 25-1b if applicable.

If a ball is believed to be lying in water in a *water hazard*, the player may probe for it with a club or otherwise. If the ball is moved in so doing, no penalty is incurred; the ball shall be replaced, unless the player elects to proceed under Rule 26-1.

PENALTY FOR BREACH OF RULE 12-1:

Match play — Loss of hole; Stroke play — Two strokes.

12-2 IDENTIFYING BALL

The responsibility for playing the proper ball rests with the player. Each player should put an identification mark on his ball.

Except in a *hazard*, the player may, without penalty, lift a ball he believes to be his own for the purpose of identification and clean it to the extent necessary for identification. If the ball is the player's ball, he shall replace it. Before lifting the ball, the player must announce his intention to his opponent in match play or his *marker* or a *fellow-competitor* in stroke play and mark the position of the ball. He must then give his opponent, marker or fellow-competitor an opportunity to observe the lifting and replacement. If he lifts his ball without announcing his intention in advance, marking the position of the ball or giving his opponent, marker or fellow-competitor an opportunity to observe, or if he lifts his ball for identification in a hazard, or cleans it more than necessary for identification, **he shall incur a penalty of one stroke** and the ball shall be replaced.

If a player who is required to replace a ball fails to do so, **he shall incur the penalty** for a breach of Rule 20-3a, but no additional penalty under Rule 12-2 shall be applied.

RULE 12 INCIDENT

Nick Faldo discovered the Rules' protective nuances while searching for his ball in a tree at Pebble Beach's 14th hole during the 1992 U.S. Open.

His second shot at the 565-yard par 5 finished dangerously close to the out of bounds on the right of the hole. For his third shot, Faldo selected a short iron in order to play over the singular tree, which protects the elbow of the hole's second dogleg. As the ball climbed it struck the tree, but no one saw it fall back to earth.

Faldo asked the Rules official walking with the group if a provisional ball could be played. Because the official had not seen the ball come down, he replied that Faldo was entitled to play a provisional ball as the original might well be lost.

After playing the provisional ball and as they walked toward the tree to look for the original ball, Faldo asked the Rules official if it was

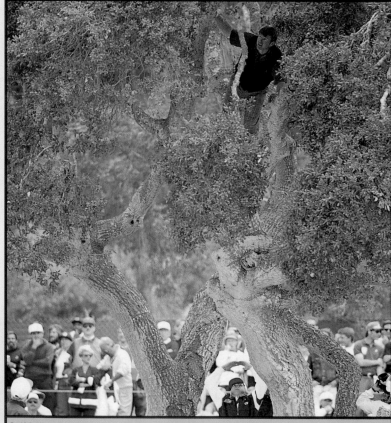

Golf balls can come to rest in some odd places. At the 1992 U.S. Open, Nick Faldo scaled a tree in search of his ball that had apparently come to rest there. See the story above.

permissible to climb the tree in order to search for his ball. The official advised that it was permissible, but cautioned him that if the ball moved while Faldo looked for it he would incur a penalty stroke and the ball would have to be replaced. Decision 18-2a/26 states exactly that.

However, the Rules official further advised Faldo that, if he stated his intention to declare his ball unplayable should he find it but before climbing or shaking the tree, there would be no penalty for moving the ball during the search. With such a prior notification, one penalty stroke would be assessed for a ball unplayable but no additional penalty would be incurred for moving the ball as provided in Decision 18-2a/27.

Faldo listened to the advice, declared that should he find his ball he intended to proceed under the unplayable ball Rule, and then climbed the tree to search for it. Having no luck, he shook the tree in hopes of dislodging the ball. It did not appear.

Unable to find his original ball, Faldo's provisional ball became the ball in play under penalty of stroke and distance.

RULE **13** BALL PLAYED AS IT LIES

DEFINITIONS

A **hazard** is any *bunker* or *water hazard*.

A **bunker** is a *hazard* consisting of a prepared area of ground, often a hollow, from which turf or soil has been removed and replaced with sand or the like. Grass-covered ground bordering or within a bunker is not part of the bunker. The margin of a bunker extends vertically downwards, but not upwards. A ball is in a bunker when it lies in or any part of it touches the bunker.

A **water hazard** is any sea, lake, pond, river, ditch, surface drainage ditch or other open water course (whether or not containing water) and anything of a similar nature.

All ground or water within the margin of a water hazard is part of the water hazard. The margin of a water hazard extends vertically upwards and downwards. Stakes and lines defining the margins of water hazards are in the hazards. Such stakes are *obstructions*. A ball is in a water hazard when it lies in or any part of it touches the water hazard.

Note 1: Water hazards (other than *lateral water hazards*) should be defined by yellow stakes or lines.

Note 2: The *Committee* may make a Local Rule prohibiting play from an environmentally-sensitive area which has been defined as a water hazard.

The **line of play** is the direction which the player wishes his ball to take after a *stroke*, plus a reasonable distance on either side of the intended direction. The line of play extends vertically upwards from the ground, but does not extend beyond the *hole*.

Taking the **stance** consists in a player placing his feet in position for and preparatory to making a *stroke*.

51

13-1 GENERAL

The ball shall be played as it lies, except as otherwise provided in the Rules. (Ball at rest moved — see Rule 18).

13-2 IMPROVING LIE, AREA OF INTENDED STANCE OR SWING, OR LINE OF PLAY

See **incident** involving Rule 13-2 on page 54

Except as provided in the *Rules*, a player shall not improve or allow to be improved:

the position or lie of his ball,
the area of his intended stance or swing,
his *line of play* or a reasonable extension of that line beyond the *hole*, or
the area in which he is to drop or place a ball

by any of the following actions:

moving, bending or breaking anything growing or fixed (including immovable *obstructions* and objects defining *out of bounds*),
creating or eliminating irregularities of surface,
removing or pressing down sand, loose soil, replaced divots or other cut turf placed in position, or
removing dew, frost or water

except as follows:

as may occur in fairly taking his *stance*,
in making a *stroke* or the backward movement of his club for a stroke,
on the *teeing ground* in creating or eliminating irregularities of surface, or
on the *putting green* in removing sand and loose soil as provided in Rule 16-1a or in repairing damage as provided in Rule 16-1c.

The club may be grounded only lightly and shall not be pressed on the ground.

Exception: Ball in hazard — see Rule 13-4.

IMPROVING AREA OF INTENDED SWING OR LINE OF PLAY

A player must not break an interfering branch or remove sand which is off the putting green but on the line of play.

13-3 BUILDING STANCE

A player is entitled to place his feet firmly in taking his *stance*, but he shall not build a stance.

See **incident** involving Rule 13-3 on page 55

13-4 BALL IN HAZARD

Except as provided in the *Rules*, before making a *stroke* at a ball which is in a *hazard* (whether a *bunker* or a *water hazard*) or which, having been lifted from a hazard, may be dropped or placed in the hazard, the player shall not:

a. Test the condition of the hazard or any similar hazard,

See **incident** involving Rule 13-4 on page 131

BALL IN BUNKER

Before making a stroke at a ball which is in a bunker the player shall not:

| ... touch the ground with his club | ... touch a loose impediment with his club at address or on his backswing | ... remove loose impediments | ... or smooth sand |

b. Touch the ground in the hazard or water in the water hazard with a club or otherwise, or

c. Touch or move a *loose impediment* lying in or touching the hazard.

Exceptions:

1. Provided nothing is done which constitutes testing the condition of the hazard or improves the lie of the ball, there is no penalty if the player (a) touches the ground in any hazard or water in a water hazard as a result of or to prevent falling, in removing an *obstruction*, in measuring or in retrieving, lifting, placing or replacing a ball under any Rule or (b) places his clubs in a hazard.

2. The player after playing the *stroke*, or his *caddie* at any time without the authority of the player, may smooth sand or soil in the hazard, provided that, if the ball is still in the hazard, nothing is done which improves the lie of the ball or assists the player in his subsequent play of the hole.

Note: At any time, including at address or in the backward movement for the *stroke*, the player may touch with a club or otherwise any *obstruction*, any construction declared by the *Committee* to be an integral part of the course or any grass, bush, tree or other growing thing.

PENALTY FOR BREACH OF RULE:

Match play — Loss of hole; Stroke play — Two strokes.

(Searching for ball — see Rule 12-1.)

RULE 13 INCIDENTS

Bernhard Langer, playing the 9th hole at Wentworth in the 1999 Volvo PGA Championship was uncharacteristically careless when taking a practice swing near his ball which lay in rough near some trees. In so doing, he knocked down some leaves from a tree, an act which could have cost him a two stroke penalty. The Tournament Committee interviewed the player immediately after he had completed his round and reviewed the television replay several times, latterly with the player, in order to determine whether Langer should be penalised under Rule 13-2 for improving the area of his intended swing. However, after due consideration it was decided that Langer's knocking down of leaves had not resulted in any improvement in the area of intended swing when he came to play the stroke. Consequently, he was not penalised.

In the third round of a US Tour event at Torry Pines near San Diego in 1987, when playing from underneath the branches of a tree, Craig Stadler unwittingly breached Rule 13-3 when he knelt on a towel to keep his trousers dry. Rule 13-3 states that a player is entitled to place his feet firmly in taking a stance but he must not build a stance. Prior to the incident, Decision 13-3/2 had been published stating that the act of kneeling on a towel, in such circumstances, was deemed to be building a stance.

A television viewer watching recorded coverage of the earlier rounds brought the incident to the attention of Tournament officials during the final round of the competition. Unfortunately, because Stadler had returned his score card for the third round containing a score for a hole lower than actually taken he was disqualified under Rule 6-6d.

However, in 1995 Stadler had the satisfaction of returning to Torry Pines to assist in cutting down the tree that was now dying of a fungus infection. He also recreated his stroke for the assembled media.

Craig Stadler returns to Torry Pines in 1995 and recreates the stroke
for the assembled media.

RULE **14** | STRIKING THE BALL

DEFINITION A **stroke** is the forward movement of the club made with the intention of fairly striking at and moving the ball, but if a player checks his downswing voluntarily before the clubhead reaches the ball he is deemed not to have made a stroke.

BALL TO BE FAIRLY STRUCK AT WITH CLUBHEAD

A player may strike the ball with the back or toe of the clubhead.

14-1 BALL TO BE FAIRLY STRUCK AT

The ball shall be fairly struck at with the head of the club and must not be pushed, scraped or spooned.

14-2 ASSISTANCE

See **incident** involving Rule 14-2 on page 58

In making a *stroke*, a player shall not:

a. accept physical assistance or protection from the elements, or

b. allow his *caddie*, his partner or his partner's caddie to position himself on or close to an extension of the *line of play* or the *line of putt* behind the ball.

PENALTY FOR BREACH OF RULE 14-1 or -2:
Match play — Loss of hole; Stroke play — Two strokes.

ASSISTANCE IN MAKING A STROKE

A player must not accept protection from the elements in making a stroke.

A player may protect himself from the elements in making a stroke.

CADDIE POSITIONED ON EXTENSION OF LINE OF PLAY BEHIND BALL

14-3 ARTIFICIAL DEVICES AND UNUSUAL EQUIPMENT

A player in doubt as to whether use of an item would constitute a breach of Rule 14-3 should consult the Royal and Ancient Golf Club of St. Andrews.

A manufacturer may submit to the Royal and Ancient Golf Club of St. Andrews a sample of an item which is to be manufactured for a ruling as to whether its use during a *stipulated round* would cause a player to be in breach of Rule 14-3. Such sample will become the property of the Royal and Ancient Golf Club of St. Andrews for reference purposes. If a manufacturer fails to submit a sample before manufacturing and/or marketing the item, the manufacturer assumes the risk of a ruling that use of the item would be contrary to the Rules of Golf.

Except as provided in the Rules, during a stipulated round the player shall not use any artificial device or unusual equipment:

a. Which might assist him in making a *stroke* or in his play; or

b. For the purpose of gauging or measuring distance or conditions which might affect his play; or

c. Which might assist him in gripping the club, except that:

(i)   plain gloves may be worn;

(ii) resin, powder and drying or moisturising agents may be used; and

(iii) a towel or handkerchief may be wrapped around the grip.

PENALTY FOR BREACH OF RULE 14-3:

Disqualification.

14-4 STRIKING THE BALL MORE THAN ONCE

See **incident** involving Rule 14-4 on page 58

If a player's club strikes the ball more than once in the course of a *stroke*, the player shall count the stroke and **add a penalty stroke**, making two strokes in all.

57

14-5 PLAYING MOVING BALL

A player shall not play while his ball is moving.

Exceptions:

Ball falling off tee – Rule 11-3.

Striking the ball more than once – Rule 14-4.

Ball moving in water – Rule 14-6.

When the ball begins to move only after the player has begun the *stroke* or the backward movement of his club for the stroke, he shall incur no penalty under this Rule for playing a moving ball, but he is not exempt from any penalty incurred under the following Rules:

Ball at rest moved by player – Rule 18-2a.

Ball at rest moving after address – Rule 18-2b.

Ball at rest moving after loose impediment touched – Rule 18-2c.

(Ball purposely deflected or stopped by player, partner or caddie – see Rule 1-2.)

14-6 BALL MOVING IN WATER

When a ball is moving in water in a *water hazard*, the player may, without penalty, make a *stroke*, but he must not delay making his stroke in order to allow the wind or current to improve the position of the ball. A ball moving in water in a water hazard may be lifted if the player elects to invoke Rule 26.

PENALTY FOR BREACH OF RULE 14-5 or -6:

Match play — Loss of hole; Stroke play — Two strokes.

RULE 14 INCIDENTS

On a rainy day at the 1995 British Masters at Collingtree Park, Domingo Hospital's first putt on the 11th hole, came to rest just a few inches from the hole. His caddie walked with him holding an umbrella over Hospital's head. Unfortunately, as Hospital putted out his caddie still had the umbrella over his head and, therefore, the player incurred a penalty of two strokes under Rule 14-2a for accepting protection from the elements.

If Hospital had held the umbrella himself he would not have incurred any penalty as a player may protect himself from the elements. However, he must not accept such protection from anyone else.

With 14 holes to play in the 1985 US Open T C Chen led the Championship by four strokes when his ball finished in thick rough to the right of the 5th green at Oakland Hills.

In attempting to play a delicate chip his club struck the ball twice during the stroke. In such a situation Rule 14-4 provides that the player shall count the stroke and add a penalty stroke, making two strokes in all. The second strike of the ball pushed it a little higher in the air and slightly to Chen's left. It came to rest on the apron of the putting green about ten feet from the hole. Visibly shaken, Chen took three more to finish the hole for an eight and his four stroke lead had evaporated on one hole. Indeed, he ultimately tied for second with Denis Watson and Dave Barr, just one shot behind Andy North.

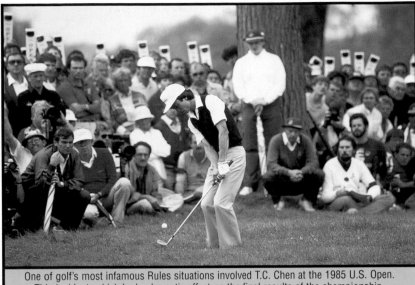

One of golf's most infamous Rules situations involved T.C. Chen at the 1985 U.S. Open.
This incident, which had a dramatic effect on the final results of the championship,
is retold on this page.

RULE 15 WRONG BALL; SUBSTITUTED BALL

DEFINITION

A **wrong ball** is any ball other than the player's:
a. *Ball in play*,
b. *Provisional ball*, or
c. Second ball played under Rule 3-3 or Rule 20-7b in stroke play.
Note: Ball in play includes a ball substituted for the ball in play, whether or
not such substitution is permitted.

15-1 GENERAL

A player must hole out with the ball played from the *teeing ground* unless a
Rule permits him to substitute another ball. If a player substitutes another ball
when not so permitted, that ball is not a *wrong ball*; it becomes the *ball in play*
and, if the error is not corrected as provided in Rule 20-6, **the player shall incur
a penalty of loss of hole in match play or two strokes in stroke play.**
(Playing from wrong place — see Rule 20–7.)

15-2 MATCH PLAY

If a player plays a *stroke* with a *wrong ball* except in a *hazard*, **he shall
lose the hole**.
  If a player plays any strokes in a hazard with a wrong ball, there is no
penalty. Strokes played in a hazard with a wrong ball do not count in the
player's score. If the wrong ball belongs to another player, its owner shall
place a ball on the spot from which the wrong ball was first played.
  If the player and opponent exchange balls during the play of a hole, the
first to play the wrong ball other than from a hazard shall lose the hole;
when this cannot be determined, the hole shall be played out with the
balls exchanged.

59

See **incident**
involving Rule 15-3
on page 61

15-3 STROKE PLAY

If a competitor plays a *stroke* or strokes with a *wrong ball*, **he shall incur a penalty of two strokes**, unless the only stroke or strokes played with such ball were played when it was in a *hazard*, in which case no penalty is incurred.

The competitor must correct his mistake by playing the correct ball. If he fails to correct his mistake before he plays a stroke from the next *teeing ground* or, in the case of the last hole of the round, fails to declare his intention to correct his mistake before leaving the *putting green*, **he shall be disqualified**.

Strokes played by a competitor with a wrong ball do not count in his score.

If the wrong ball belongs to another competitor, its owner shall place a ball on the spot from which the wrong ball was first played.

(Lie of ball to be placed or replaced altered — see Rule 20-3b.)

RULE 15 INCIDENT

Nick Faldo turned a bad day into a disaster during the first round of the 1994 Open Championship at Turnberry. Two over par coming to the 17th hole, the weather deteriorated as Faldo was about to play from the tee. The driving rain and strong winds may go some way to explaining Faldo's errant shot and the fact that he did not see where his ball finished. Both Faldo and his fellow-competitor Jim McGovern pushed their drives into the right rough but Faldo's drive was shorter and wider than McGovern's. Faldo found a ball short of where McGovern was looking for his and played it.

However, Faldo had not checked that the ball was his before playing it, which seemed totally out of character for a player so meticulous in his approach to the game. Just a glimpse at the ball would have shown that it was not his but McGovern's as McGovern was playing a different brand.

Subsequent to Faldo playing his stroke, McGovern was advised that the other ball was in deep rough, something which confused him until he reached it, and saw that it belonged to Faldo. The mistake cost Faldo a two-stroke penalty under Rule 15-3 and, as required by this Rule, he had to correct his error by playing his own ball. Faldo completed the hole with a three over par 8, and his round in 75.

Faldo's mood certainly improved by the end of the week, a second round 66 meant that he made the cut and this score was improved on the final day with a 64 giving him a four round total of 275, 5 under par and a share of 8th place.

RULE 16 THE PUTTING GREEN

DEFINITIONS

The **putting green** is all ground of the hole being played which is specially prepared for putting or otherwise defined as such by the *Committee*. A ball is on the putting green when any part of it touches the putting green.

The **line of putt** is the line which the player wishes his ball to take after a *stroke* on the *putting green*. Except with respect to Rule 16-1e, the line of putt includes a reasonable distance on either side of the intended line. The line of putt does not extend beyond the *hole*.

TOUCHING LINE OF PUTT: EXAMPLES OF WHEN PERMITTED

addressing the ball

removing a loose impediment

repairing a ball mark

repairing an old hole plug

A ball is **holed** when it is at rest within the circumference of the *hole* and all of it is below the level of the lip of the hole.

16-1 GENERAL
a Touching Line of Putt
The *line of putt* must not be touched except:
(i)   the player may move sand and loose soil on the *putting green* and other *loose impediments* by picking them up or by brushing them aside with his hand or a club without pressing anything down;

PROCEDURE FOR MARKING THE BALL

Do I have to use a ball-marker to mark my ball?

No. Although you are recommended to use a ball-marker or small coin, you may use something else like a tee or the putter head.

(ii)   in *addressing the ball*, the player may place the club in front of the ball without pressing anything down;

(iii)   in measuring — Rule 10-4;

(iv)   in lifting the ball — Rule 16-1b;

(v)   in pressing down a ball-marker;

(vi)   in repairing old hole plugs or ball marks on the putting green — Rule 16-1c; and

(vii) in removing movable *obstructions* — Rule 24-1.

(Indicating line for putting on putting green — see Rule 8-2b.)

b Lifting Ball

A ball on the *putting green* may be lifted and, if desired, cleaned.

A ball so lifted shall be replaced on the spot from which it was lifted.

c Repair of Hole Plugs, Ball Marks and Other Damage

The player may repair an old hole plug or damage to the *putting green* caused by the impact of a ball, whether or not the player's ball lies on the putting green. If a ball or ball-marker is accidentally moved in the process of such repair, the ball or ball marker shall be replaced, without penalty. Any other damage to the putting green shall not be repaired if it might assist the player in his subsequent play of the hole.

d Testing Surface

During the play of a hole, a player shall not test the surface of the *putting green* by rolling a ball or roughening or scraping the surface.

e Standing Astride or On Line of Putt

The player shall not make a *stroke* on the *putting green* from a *stance* astride, or with either foot touching, the *line of putt* or an extension of that line behind the ball.

A player may not repair spike damage if it might subsequently assist him.

A player may clean a ball by rubbing it on the green, provided he doesn't test the green's surface. However, such a method of cleaning a ball is not recommended - Decision 16-1d/5.

f Playing Stroke While Another Ball in Motion

The player shall not play a *stroke* while another ball is in motion after a stroke from the *putting green*, except that, if a player does so, he incurs no penalty if it was his turn to play.

(Lifting ball interfering with or assisting play while another ball in motion — see Rule 22.)

PENALTY FOR BREACH OF RULE 16-1:

Match play — Loss of hole; Stroke play — Two strokes.

(Position of *caddie* or *partner* — see Rule 14-2.)

(*Wrong putting green* — see Rule 25-3.)

16-2 BALL OVERHANGING HOLE

See **incidents** involving Rule 16-2 on page 65

When any part of the ball overhangs the lip of the hole, the player is allowed enough time to reach the hole without unreasonable delay and an additional ten seconds to determine whether the ball is at rest. If by then the ball has not fallen into the hole, it is deemed to be at rest. If the ball subsequently falls into the hole, the player is deemed to have holed out with his last stroke, and **he shall add a penalty stroke to his score** for the hole; otherwise there is no penalty under this Rule.

(Undue delay — see Rule 6-7.)

BALL OVERHANGING HOLE

How long may I wait to see if my ball will fall into the hole?

There's no point in waiting more than ten seconds. After that time the ball is deemed to be at rest and if it then falls in you have holed out with your last stroke, but you add a penalty stroke.

RULE 16 INCIDENTS

The Rule dealing with a ball overhanging the hole was revised as a result of an incident involving Denis Watson during play of the 8th hole in the first round of the 1985 U.S. Open at Oakland Hills Country Club.

From 10 feet, Watson putted and his ball stopped on the lip of the hole. After waiting an extended period of time, the ball fell in. Subsequently, Watson was told to add two penalty strokes to his score for undue delay as described at the time in Rule 16-1h.

The severe ramification of the penalty would not be clear for three more days when Watson would finish just one stroke behind the champion, Andy North.

In 1988, the Rule was moved to Rule 16-2 and a one-stroke penalty assigned to any breach.

The 2000 Qatar Masters highlighted the principles of Rule 16-2 in an intriguing incident involving Soren Hansen and Matthais Gronberg. Hansen's ten foot putt hovered over the edge of the hole before finally falling into the hole. Gronberg, one of Hansen's fellow-competitors announced he had been counting and since he got to 11 and the time limit was 10 seconds, he should add a penalty stroke to his score. Voices were raised above the wind and a Rules official was summoned.

After the official had listened to accounts of the incident from all witnesses he ruled that Hansen had incurred a penalty of one stroke under Rule 16-2. However, on returning to the Tournament office, the referee asked whether there was any television coverage of the incident available. Fortunately there was and this showed that, after Hansen being given a reasonable time to reach the hole, only eight seconds had elapsed when the ball fell into the hole and, consequently, the penalty was rescinded.

RULE 17 THE FLAGSTICK

DEFINITION

The **flagstick** is a movable straight indicator, with or without bunting or other material attached, centred in the hole to show its position. It shall be circular in cross-section.

17-1 FLAGSTICK ATTENDED, REMOVED OR HELD UP

Before and during the *stroke*, the player may have the *flagstick* attended, removed or held up to indicate the position of the *hole*. This may be done only on the authority of the player before he plays his stroke.

If, prior to the stroke, the flagstick is attended, removed or held up by anyone with the player's knowledge and no objection is made, the player shall be deemed to have authorised it. If anyone attends or holds up the flagstick or stands near the hole while a stroke is being played, he shall be deemed to be attending the flagstick until the ball comes to rest.

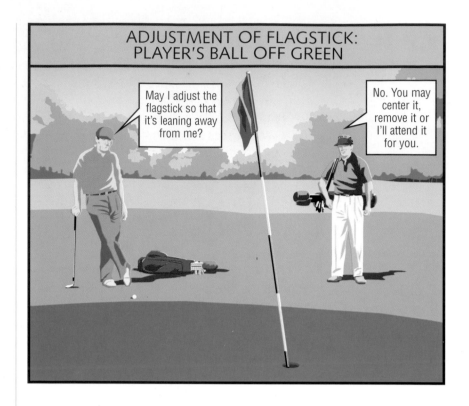

17-2 UNAUTHORISED ATTENDANCE
a Match Play

In match play, an opponent or his *caddie* shall not, without the authority or prior knowledge of the player, attend, remove or hold up the *flagstick* while the player is making a *stroke* or his ball is in motion.

b Stroke Play

In stroke play, if a *fellow-competitor* or his *caddie* attends, removes or holds up the *flagstick* without the competitor's authority or prior knowledge while the competitor is making a *stroke* or his ball is in motion, **the *fellow-competitor* shall incur the penalty** for breach of this Rule. In such circumstances, if the competitor's ball strikes the flagstick, the person attending it or anything carried by him, the competitor incurs no penalty and the ball shall be played as it lies, except that, if the stroke was played from the *putting green*, the stroke shall be cancelled, the ball replaced and the stroke replayed.

PENALTY FOR BREACH OF RULE 17-1 or -2:
Match play — Loss of hole; Stroke play — Two strokes.

17-3 BALL STRIKING FLAGSTICK OR ATTENDANT

See **incidents** involving Rule 17-3 on page 68

The player's ball shall not strike:
a. The *flagstick* when attended, removed or held up by the player, his *partner* or either of their *caddies*, or by another person with the player's authority or prior knowledge; or
b. The player's *caddie*, his partner or his partner's caddie when attending the *flagstick*, or another person attending the flagstick with the player's authority or prior knowledge or anything carried by any such person; or
c. The *flagstick* in the hole, unattended, when the ball has been played from the *putting green*.

PENALTY FOR BREACH OF RULE 17-3:
Match play — Loss of hole; Stroke play — Two strokes,
and the ball shall be played as it lies.

17-4 BALL RESTING AGAINST FLAGSTICK

If the ball rests against the *flagstick* when it is in the hole, the player or another person authorised by him may move or remove the flagstick and if the ball falls into the hole, the player shall be deemed to have holed out with his last stroke; otherwise the ball, if *moved*, shall be placed on the lip of the hole, without penalty.

RULE 17 INCIDENTS

During the 1995 Open at St Andrews, Peter Fowler of Australia, found himself on the front edge of the second green of the Old Course, with the hole in the back left corner beyond the huge humps and swales that are a feature of the green. He asked the referee if he could play the stroke with a wedge. The Rules do not stipulate that a player must use a putter when his ball is on the green and, therefore, he was given the go-ahead and pitched to within three feet of the hole.

Corey Pavin was on the other half of this double green, playing the 16th. He congratulated Fowler on a great shot, but warned; "Next time have the flag attended. It's a two-shot penalty if you hit the stick." The fact that the ball was on the green and, therefore, Rule 17-3c could have been breached, had escaped everyone else's attention.

The incident repeated itself in the 2000 Open at the same hole, this time with Jack Nicklaus. Nicklaus had hit his second shot well to the left, on the 16th hole portion of the green, with a bunker between himself and the hole on the second. He floated up a perfect wedge shot that almost went in the hole. The referee accompanying the group was unsighted by the bunker and assumed that Nicklaus had played his shot from the fairway beyond the green.

As they walked to the next tee Nicklaus admitted that he was unsure if his ball was on the green or not and the referee reminded him that if he had played from the green he should have had the flag attended.

"I had a 40 yard pitch shot over a bunker," said Nicklaus after the round "You don't think much about having the pin attended. I've never done that before. It never entered my mind."

Miguel Angel Jimenez found himself in an awkward situation on Pebble Beach's 17th green during the 2000 U.S. Open. When the course was altered in 1929 the 17th green was redesigned into a large hourglass shape divided by a diagonal ridge. The ridge running through its centre makes it play like a double green. Hence, when the hole is cut at back left, it is difficult for a ball played from front right to get close to the hole. This was Jimenez's dilemma.

The pinched, hourglass shape brought the rough into the line of putt necessary for him to get close to the hole. For this reason, he chose to play a pitch shot from over the rough and over the ridge to the hole on the other side of the green.

Jimenez was aware of the Rules regarding the flagstick, but he wisely sought confirmation from the referee walking with his group.

Rule 17-3 states that a player's ball shall not strike the flagstick in the hole, unattended, when the ball has been played from the green. In order to avoid such a breach of the Rules, Jimenez directed his caddie to attend the flagstick.

Therefore, Jimenez's caddie would be required to remove the flagstick if it looked as though the ball might go in the hole.

Playing a delicate pitch, Jimenez took a small divot. His ball landed on the down slope of the ridge and ran to about 10 feet from the hole. From there he took two putts for bogey.

RULE **18** BALL AT REST MOVED

DEFINITIONS

A ball is deemed to have **moved** if it leaves its position and comes to rest in any other place.

An **outside agency** is any agency not part of the match or, in stroke play, not part of the competitor's *side*, and includes a *referee*, a *marker*, an *observer* and a *forecaddie*. Neither wind nor water is an outside agency.

Equipment is anything used, worn or carried by or for the player except any ball he has played at the hole being played and any small object, such as a coin or a tee, when used to mark the position of a ball or the extent of an area in which a ball is to be dropped. Equipment includes a golf cart, whether or not motorised. If such a cart is shared by two or more players, the cart and everything in it are deemed to be the equipment of the player whose ball is involved except that, when the cart is being moved by one of the players sharing it, the cart and everything in it are deemed to be that player's equipment.

Note: A ball played at the hole being played is equipment when it has been lifted and not put back into play.

A player has **addressed the ball** when he has taken his *stance* and has also grounded his club, except that in a *hazard* a player has addressed the ball when he has taken his stance.

Taking the **stance** consists in a player placing his feet in position for and preparatory to making a *stroke*.

18-1 BY OUTSIDE AGENCY

See **incident** involving Rule 18-1 on page 114

If a ball at rest is moved by an *outside agency*, the player shall incur no penalty and the ball shall be replaced before the player plays another *stroke*. (Player's ball at rest *moved* by another ball — see Rule 18-5.)

18-2 BY PLAYER, PARTNER, CADDIE OR EQUIPMENT
a General

See **incidents** involving Rule 18-2a on page 72

When a player's ball is *in play*, if:

(i) the player, his *partner* or either of their *caddies* lifts or *moves* it, touches it purposely (except with a club in the act of addressing it) or causes it to *move* except as permitted by a *Rule*, or

69

BALL AT REST MOVED

By Outside Agency -
no penalty and
replace ball
(Rule 18-1)

**By Player, Partner,
Caddie or Equipment -**
one stroke penalty
and replace ball
(Rule 18-2a)

After Address -
one stroke penalty
and replace ball
(Rule 18-2b)

**After Loose
Impediment Touched -**
if loose impediment
within one club-length
of ball, one stroke
penalty and
replace ball
(Rule 18-2c)

**By Opponent,
Caddie or Equipment
During Search -**
no penalty and
replace ball
(Rule 18-3a)

**By Opponent,
Caddie or Equipment
Not During Search -**
opponent incurs
one stroke penalty and
replace ball
(Rule 18-3b)

**By Fellow-Competitor,
Caddie or Equipment
-**
no penalty and
replace ball
(Rule18-4)

By Another Ball -
replace moved ball
(Rule 18-5)

(ii) *equipment* of the player or his *partner* causes the ball to *move*, **the player shall incur a penalty stroke**. The ball shall be replaced unless the movement of the ball occurs after the player has begun his swing and he does not discontinue his swing.

Under the *Rules* no penalty is incurred if a player accidentally causes his ball to move in the following circumstances:

In measuring to determine which ball farther from hole — Rule 10-4

In searching for covered ball in *hazard* or for ball in an *abnormal ground condition* — Rule 12-1

In the process of repairing hole plug or ball mark — Rule 16-1c

In the process of removing *loose impediments* on *putting green* — Rule 18-2c

In the process of lifting ball under a Rule — Rule 20-1.

In the process of placing or replacing ball under a Rule — Rule 20-3a

In removal of movable *obstruction* — Rule 24-1

b Ball Moving After Address

See **incident** involving Rule 18-2b on page 72

If a player's *ball in play moves* after he has *addressed* it (other than as a result of a *stroke*), the player shall be deemed to have moved the ball and **shall incur a penalty stroke**. The player shall replace the ball unless the movement of the ball occurs after he has begun his swing and he does not discontinue his swing.

c Ball Moving After Loose Impediment Touched

Through the green, if the ball *moves* after any *loose impediment*, lying within a club-length of it has been touched by the player, his *partner* or either of their *caddies* and before the player has *addressed* it, the player shall be deemed to have moved the ball and **shall incur a *penalty stroke***. The player shall replace the ball unless the movement of the ball occurs after he has begun his swing and he does not discontinue his swing.

On the *putting green*, if the ball or the ball-marker moves in the process of removing any loose impediment, the ball or the ball-marker shall be replaced. There is no penalty provided the movement of the ball or the ball-marker is directly attributable to the removal of the loose impediment. Otherwise, **the player shall incur a *penalty stroke*** under Rule 18-2a or 20-1.

18-3 BY OPPONENT, CADDIE OR EQUIPMENT IN MATCH PLAY
a During Search

If, during search for a player's ball, the ball is *moved* by an opponent, his *caddie* or his *equipment*, no penalty is incurred and the player shall replace the ball.

b Other Than During Search

If, other than during search for a ball, the ball is touched or *moved* by an opponent, his *caddie* or his *equipment*, except as otherwise provided in the *Rules*, **the opponent shall incur a penalty stroke**. The player shall replace the ball.

(Ball moved in measuring to determine which ball farther from the *hole* — see Rule 10-4.)

(Playing a wrong ball — see Rule 15-2.)

18-4 BY FELLOW-COMPETITOR, CADDIE OR EQUIPMENT IN STROKE PLAY

If a competitor's ball is *moved* by a *fellow-competitor*, his *caddie* or his *equipment*, no penalty is incurred. The competitor shall replace his ball. (Playing a wrong *ball* — see Rule 15-3.)

18-5 BY ANOTHER BALL

If a *ball in play* and at rest is *moved* by another ball in motion after a *stroke*, the moved ball shall be replaced.

*PENALTY FOR BREACH OF RULE:

Match play — Loss of hole; Stroke play — Two strokes.

*If a player who is required to replace a ball fails to do so, he shall incur the general penalty for breach of Rule 18 but no additional penalty under Rule 18 shall be applied.

Note 1: If a ball to be replaced under this Rule is not immediately recoverable, another ball may be substituted.

Note 2: If it is impossible to determine the spot on which a ball is to be placed, see Rule 20-3c.

RULE 18 INCIDENTS

At the 1925 U.S. Open Championship at Worcester Country Club in Massachusetts, Bobby Jones saw his ball move after he addressed it on a steep bank at the 11th hole during the first round. Jones insisted that a penalty be added to his score. Often the player may be the only one who sees such a breach and, in such circumstances, must call the penalty on himself.

When praised for his honesty, Jones replied, "You just might as well praise me for not breaking into banks. There is only one way to play this game."

Jones began the final round in a tie for fourth place but was able to tie Willie Macfarlane to force a 36-hole play-off, which he lost by one stroke.

While executing his pre-shot routine before putting at the 17th hole in the 1997 Players Championship, David Love III's putter accidentally moved his ball about a foot. Failing to replace the moved ball, he two putted and went to the 18th tee. Assessing himself one stroke for moving his ball rather than the total penalty of two strokes for moving and not replacing his ball, Love recorded a four on his score card instead of a five.

Although viewed by thousands in person, the error was not brought to Love's attention until after his score card had been returned. The result was disqualification under Rule 6-6d for returning a score for a hole lower than actually taken.

On a particularly windy day at Royal Birkdale during the 1998 Open Championship, Per-Ulrik Johannson had played a good shot to the 8th green and was preparing to putt when a gust of wind caused his ball to move.

Immediately turning to the referee for assistance, he explained that the ball moved after he had placed his club behind the ball but before he had placed his feet in position for putting. The referee had to ascertain whether Johannson had completed his address procedure because, even though the wind had moved the ball, if the player had addressed it prior to this occurring he would be deemed to have moved it under Rule 18-2b, resulting in a one stroke penalty. Fortunately for Johannson, it was determined that at the time the ball moved he had not completed taking his stance and, therefore, in accordance with the Definition he had not addressed the ball. Therefore, he incurred no penalty and was required to play the ball from its new position.

RULE **19**

BALL IN MOTION DEFLECTED OR STOPPED

DEFINITIONS

An **outside agency** is any agency not part of the match or, in stroke play, not part of the competitor's side, and includes a *referee*, a *marker*, an *observer* and a *forecaddie*. Neither wind nor water is an outside agency.

Equipment is anything used, worn or carried by or for the player except any ball he has played at the hole being played and any small object, such as a coin or a tee, when used to mark the position of a ball or the extent of an area in which a ball is to be dropped. Equipment includes a golf cart, whether or not motorised. If such a cart is shared by two or more players, the cart and everything in it are deemed to be the equipment of the player whose ball is involved except that, when the cart is being moved by one of the players sharing it, the cart and everything in it are deemed to be that player's equipment.

Note: A ball played at the hole being played is equipment when it has been lifted and not put back into play.

See **incident** involving Rule 19-1 on page 77

19-1 BY OUTSIDE AGENCY

If a ball in motion is accidentally deflected or stopped by any *outside agency*, it is a *rub of the green*, no penalty is incurred and the ball shall be played as it lies except:

a. If a ball in motion after a *stroke* other than on the *putting green* comes to rest in or on any moving or animate *outside agency*, the player shall, *through the green* or in a *hazard*, drop the ball, or on the putting green place the ball, as near as possible to the spot where the outside agency was when the ball came to rest in or on it, and

b. If a ball in motion after a *stroke* on the *putting green* is deflected or stopped by, or comes to rest in or on, any moving or animate *outside agency* except a worm or an insect, the stroke shall be cancelled, the ball replaced and the stroke replayed.

If the ball is not immediately recoverable, another ball may be substituted.

73

BALL IN MOTION DEFLECTED OR STOPPED

By Player, Partner, Caddie or Equipment Match Play - player loses hole (Rule 19-2a)

By Player, Partner, Caddie or Equipment Stroke Play - player incurs penalty of two strokes and ball played as it lies (Rule 19-2b)

By Outside Agency - no penalty and ball played as it lies (Rule 19-1)

By Opponent, Caddie or Equipment Match Play - no penalty and ball played as it lies or stroke cancelled and replayed (Rule 19-3)

By Fellow-Competitor, Caddie or Equipment Stroke Play - see Rule 19-1 regarding ball deflected by Outside Agency (Rule 19-4)

By Another Ball at Rest - no penalty and ball played as it lies. Except in stroke play, if both balls lay on green prior to stroke, player incurs two stroke penalty (Rule 19-5a)

By Another Ball in Motion - no penalty and ball played as it lies, unless player in breach of Rule 16-1f (Rule 19-5b)

Player's ball deflected or stopped by another ball — see Rule 19-5.)
Note: If the *referee* or the *Committee* determines that a player's ball has been purposely deflected or stopped by an *outside agency*, Rule 1-4 applies to the player. If the outside agency is a *fellow-competitor* or his *caddie*, Rule 1-2 applies to the fellow-competitor.

19-2 BY PLAYER, PARTNER, CADDIE OR EQUIPMENT
a Match Play

See **incident** involving Rule 19-2 on page 77

If a player's ball is accidentally deflected or stopped by himself, his *partner* or either of their *caddies* or *equipment*, **he shall lose the hole**.

b Stroke Play
If a competitor's ball is accidentally deflected or stopped by himself, his *partner* or either of their *caddies* or *equipment*, **the competitor shall incur a penalty of two strokes**. The ball shall be played as it lies, except when it comes to rest in or on the competitor's, his partner's or either of their caddies' clothes or equipment, in which case the competitor shall *through the green* or in a *hazard* drop the ball, or on the *putting green* place the ball, as near as possible to where the article was when the ball came to rest in or on it.
Exception: Dropped Ball — see Rule 20-2a.
(Ball purposely deflected or stopped by player, partner or caddie — see Rule 1-2.)

19-3 BY OPPONENT, CADDIE OR EQUIPMENT IN MATCH PLAY
If a player's ball is accidentally deflected or stopped by an opponent, his *caddie* or his *equipment*, no penalty is incurred. The player may play the ball as it lies or, before another *stroke* is played by either side, cancel the stroke and play a ball without penalty as nearly as possible at the spot from which the original ball was last played (see Rule 20-5).

If the ball has come to rest in or on the opponent's or his caddie's clothes or equipment, the player may *through the green* or in a *hazard* drop the ball, or on the *putting green* place the ball, as near as possible to where the article was when the ball came to rest in or on it.
Exception: Ball striking person attending flagstick — see Rule 17-3b.
(Ball purposely deflected or stopped by opponent or caddie — see Rule 1-2.)

19-4 BY FELLOW-COMPETITOR, CADDIE OR EQUIPMENT IN STROKE PLAY
See Rule 19-1 regarding ball deflected by *outside agency*.

19-5 BY ANOTHER BALL
a At Rest
If a player's ball in motion after a *stroke* is deflected or stopped by a *ball in play* and at rest, the player shall play his ball as it lies. In match play, no penalty is incurred. In stroke play, there is no penalty unless both balls lay on the *putting green* prior to the stroke, in which case **the player incurs a penalty of two strokes**.

b In Motion
If a player's ball in motion after a *stroke* is deflected or stopped by another

ball in motion after a stroke, the player shall play his ball as it lies. There is no penalty unless the player was in breach of Rule 16-1f, in which case **he shall incur the penalty for breach of that Rule**.

Exception: If the player's ball is in motion after a *stroke* on the *putting green* and the other ball in motion is an *outside agency* — see Rule 19-1b.

PENALTY FOR BREACH OF RULE:
Match play — Loss of hole; Stroke play — Two strokes.

RULE 19 INCIDENTS

In the last round of the 1990 Australian Open Brett Ogle was just two shots off the lead playing the 17th hole. In an attempt to close the deficit he risked a difficult second shot around a tree with a 2 iron. Unfortunately, his ball struck the tree situated immediately in front of him and rebounded backwards striking Ogle on the knee.

Apart from being extremely painful, Ogle suffered the indignity of a two stroke penalty under Rule 19-2 because the ball had struck him. Decision 6-8a/3 states that it is reasonable to allow a player ten or fifteen minutes to recuperate from such a physical problem. After being allowed time to recover, Ogle limped down the closing two holes, using

In the final round of the 1990 Australian Open Brett Ogle incurred an injury and a two stroke penalty for a breach of Rule 19-2.

his driver as a walking stick, followed by a team of helpers carrying bandages and ice packs behind him. He finished the 17th hole in 9 strokes, the ricochet costing him any chance of winning the title.

Ogle was in considerable pain on the Sunday night and an X-ray revealed a stellate fracture of the patella bone just below the knee.

Sergio Garcia encountered an unusual situation when his drive at Pebble Beach's 4th hole struck and killed a seagull during the second round of the 2000 U.S. Open.

The bird swooped down into the ball's path just 20 yards from the teeing ground. Travelling with great velocity, the ball struck the bird in the chest. The gull was killed. Somehow, the ball continued on in a decelerated way until it struck the top of the out of bounds fence, which shelters the beach club car park to the right of the hole. One bounce atop the picket fence and the ball was deflected back onto the course, where it settled in the rough.

Garcia was distraught by the bird's death and the bizarre rub of the green. In such a situation, no penalty is incurred and the ball must be played as it lies. At first, many of the assembled spectators thought such a ruling was unfair and Garcia should be allowed to replay the shot. Their concern was assuaged when it was pointed out that had Garcia's ball been deflected into the hole it would have been a hole-in-one.

RULE **20**

LIFTING, DROPPING AND PLACING; PLAYING FROM WRONG PLACE

See **incident** involving Rule 20-1 on page 84

20-1 LIFTING AND MARKING

A ball to be lifted under the *Rules* may be lifted by the player, his partner or another person authorised by the player. In any such case, the player shall be responsible for any breach of the Rules.

The position of the ball shall be marked before it is lifted under a Rule which requires it to be replaced. If it is not marked, **the player shall incur a penalty of one stroke** and the ball shall be replaced. If it is not replaced, the player shall incur the general penalty for breach of this Rule but no additional penalty under Rule 20-1 shall be applied.

If a ball or ball-marker is accidentally moved in the process of lifting the ball under a Rule or marking its position, the ball or the ball-marker shall be replaced. There is no penalty provided the movement of the ball or the ball-marker is directly attributable to the specific act of marking the position of or lifting the ball. Otherwise, **the player shall incur a penalty stroke** under this Rule or Rule 18-2a.

Exception: If a player incurs a penalty for failing to act in accordance with Rule 5-3 or 12-2, no additional penalty under Rule 20-1 shall be applied.

Note: The position of a ball to be lifted should be marked by placing a ball-marker, a small coin or other similar object immediately behind the ball.

77

If the ball-marker interferes with the play, *stance* or *stroke* of another player, it should be placed one or more clubhead-lengths to one side.

20-2 DROPPING AND RE-DROPPING
a By Whom and How

See **incident** involving Rule 20-2a on page 83

A ball to be dropped under the *Rules* shall be dropped by the player himself. He shall stand erect, hold the ball at shoulder height and arm's length and drop it. If a ball is dropped by any other person or in any other manner and the error is not corrected as provided in Rule 20-6, **the player shall incur a penalty stroke**.

If the ball touches the player, his partner, either of their *caddies* or their *equipment* before or after it strikes a part of the *course*, the ball shall be re-dropped, without penalty. There is no limit to the number of times a ball shall be re-dropped in such circumstances.

(Taking action to influence position or movement of ball — see Rule 1-2.)

b Where to Drop

When a ball is to be dropped as near as possible to a specific spot, it shall be dropped not nearer the hole than the specific spot which, if it is not precisely known to the player, shall be estimated.

A ball when dropped must first strike a part of the *course* where the applicable *Rule* requires it to be dropped. If it is not so dropped, Rules 20-6 and -7 apply.

c When to Re-Drop

A dropped ball shall be re-dropped without penalty if it:

(i)   rolls into and comes to rest in a *hazard*;

(ii)   rolls out of and comes to rest outside a *hazard*;

(iii) rolls onto and comes to rest on a *putting green*;

See **incident** involving Rule 20-2c on page 83

(iv)   rolls and comes to rest *out of bounds*;

(v)   rolls to and comes to rest in a position where there is interference by the condition from which relief was taken under Rule 24-2b (immovable obstruction), Rule 25-1 (abnormal ground conditions), Rule 25-3 (wrong putting green) or a Local Rule (Rule 33-8a), or rolls back into the pitch-mark from which it was lifted under Rule 25-2 (embedded ball);

(vi)   rolls and comes to rest more than two club-lengths from where it first struck a part of the course; or

(vii)   rolls and comes to rest nearer the hole than:

    a.   its original position or estimated position (see Rule 20-2b) unless otherwise permitted by the *Rules*; or

    b.   the nearest point of relief or maximum available relief (Rule 24-2, 25-1 or 25-3); or

    c.   the point where the original ball last crossed the margin of the *water hazard* or *lateral water hazard* (Rule 26-1).

If the ball when re-dropped rolls into any position listed above, it shall be placed as near as possible to the spot where it first struck a part of the course when re-dropped.

If a ball to be re-dropped or placed under this Rule is not immediately recoverable, another ball may be substituted.

Note: If a ball when dropped or re-dropped comes to rest and subsequently *moves*, the ball shall be played as it lies, unless the provisions of any other *Rule* apply.

20-3   PLACING AND REPLACING
a   By Whom and Where

A ball to be placed under the *Rules* shall be placed by the player or his partner. If a ball is to be replaced, the player, his partner or the person who lifted or moved it shall place it on the spot from which it was lifted or moved. In any such case, the player shall be responsible for any breach of the Rules.

If a ball or ball-marker is accidentally *moved* in the process of placing or replacing the ball, the ball or the ball-marker shall be replaced. There is no penalty provided the movement of the ball or the ball-marker is directly attributable to the specific act of placing or replacing the ball or removing the ball-marker. Otherwise, **the player shall incur a penalty stroke** under Rule 18-2a or 20-1.

b Lie of Ball to be Placed or Replaced Altered

If the original lie of a ball to be placed or replaced has been altered:

(i)   except in a *hazard,* the ball shall be placed in the nearest lie most similar to the original lie which is not more than one club-length from the original lie, not nearer the hole and not in a hazard;

(ii) in a *water hazard*, the ball shall be placed in accordance with Clause (i) above, except that the ball must be placed in the water hazard;

(iii) in a *bunker*, the original lie shall be recreated as nearly as possible and the ball shall be placed in that lie.

c Spot Not Determinable

See **incident** involving Rule 20-3c on page 114

If it is impossible to determine the spot where the ball is to be placed or replaced:

(i)   *through the green*, the ball shall be dropped as near as possible to the place where it lay but not in a *hazard* or on a *putting green*;

(ii) in a *hazard*, the ball shall be dropped in the *hazard* as near as possible to the place where it lay;

(iii) on the *putting green*, the ball shall be placed as near as possible to the place where it lay but not in a *hazard*.

81

See **incident** involving Rule 20-3d on page 86

d Ball Fails to Come to Rest on Spot

If a ball when placed fails to come to rest on the spot on which it was placed, it shall be replaced without penalty. If it still fails to come to rest on that spot:

(i) except in a *hazard*, it shall be placed at the nearest spot where it can be placed at rest which is not nearer the hole and not in a hazard;

(ii) in a hazard, it shall be placed in the hazard at the nearest spot where it can be placed at rest which is not nearer the hole.

If a ball when placed comes to rest on the spot on which it is placed, and it subsequently *moves*, there is no penalty and the ball shall be played as it lies, unless the provisions of any other *Rule* apply.

PENALTY FOR BREACH OF RULE 20-1, -2 or -3:
Match play — Loss of hole; Stroke play — Two strokes.

20-4 WHEN BALL DROPPED OR PLACED IS IN PLAY

If the player's *ball in play* has been lifted, it is again in play when dropped or placed.

A substituted ball becomes the ball in play when it has been dropped or placed.

(Ball incorrectly substituted — see Rule 15-1.)

(Lifting ball incorrectly substituted, dropped or placed — see Rule 20-6.)

20-5 PLAYING NEXT STROKE FROM WHERE PREVIOUS STROKE PLAYED

When, under the *Rules*, a player elects or is required to play his next *stroke* from where a previous stroke was played, he shall proceed as follows: if the stroke is to be played from the *teeing ground*, the ball to be played shall be played from anywhere within the teeing ground and may be teed; if the stroke is to be played from *through the green* or a *hazard*, it shall be dropped; if the stroke is to be played on the *putting green*, it shall be placed.

PENALTY FOR BREACH OF RULE 20-5:
Match play — Loss of hole; Stroke play — Two strokes.

20-6 LIFTING BALL INCORRECTLY SUBSTITUTED, DROPPED OR PLACED

A ball incorrectly substituted, dropped or placed in a wrong place or otherwise not in accordance with the *Rules* but not played may be lifted, without penalty, and the player shall then proceed correctly.

20-7 PLAYING FROM WRONG PLACE

For a ball played from outside the *teeing ground* or from a wrong teeing ground — see Rule 11-4 and -5.

a Match Play

If a player plays a *stroke* with a ball which has been dropped or placed in a wrong place, **he shall lose the hole**.

b Stroke Play

If a competitor plays a *stroke* with his *ball in play* (i) which has been

PLAYING FROM WRONG PLACE

If a player moves his ball-marker a putter head length to one side, he must remember to put it back before he putts. Otherwise, the player will be penalised for playing from a wrong place.

dropped or placed in a wrong place or (ii) which has been *moved* and not replaced in a case where the *Rules* require replacement, **he shall**, provided a serious breach has not occurred, **incur the penalty prescribed by the applicable Rule** and play out the hole with the ball.

If, after playing from a wrong place, a competitor becomes aware of that fact and believes that a serious breach may be involved, he may, provided he has not played a stroke from the next *teeing ground* or, in the case of the last hole of the round, left the *putting green*, declare that he will play out the hole with a second ball dropped or placed in accordance with the Rules. The competitor shall report the facts to the *Committee* before returning his score card; if he fails to do so, **he shall be disqualified**. The Committee shall determine whether a serious breach of the Rule occurred. If so, the score with the second ball shall count and **the competitor shall add two penalty strokes to his score with that ball**.

If a serious breach has occurred and the competitor has failed to correct it as prescribed above, **he shall be disqualified**.

Note: If a competitor plays a second ball, *penalty strokes* incurred solely by playing the ball ruled not to count and *strokes* subsequently taken with that ball shall be disregarded.

RULE 20 INCIDENTS

While playing the par 5 second hole at Augusta in the third round of the 1995 Masters, Nick Faldo hit his drive into the pine trees, his ball coming to rest in a ditch marked as a lateral water hazard. Faldo elected to follow the procedure prescribed in Rule 26-1c by dropping his ball within two club-lengths of where the ball last crossed the margin of the hazard.

On dropping, the ball struck Faldo's foot and rolled back into the hazard. Unsure of the correct procedure, Faldo called for a Rules official. Rule 20-2a provides that in such a case where a dropped ball touches the player before or after it strikes part of the course, the ball shall be re-dropped, without penalty. There is no limit to the number of times a ball shall be re-dropped in such circumstances, as it is effectively a "no drop". Therefore, when Faldo's second attempt at dropping the ball rolled into the hazard he was required to drop the ball a third time. When re-dropped the ball rolled and came to rest in the hazard again, so Faldo then had to place the ball on the spot where it first struck the ground when re-dropped.

In the 1999 Greg Norman Holden International at The Lakes Golf Club in Sydney, Bernhard Langer, needing a par 3 at the final hole to win missed the green and then played a poor chip to leave himself a 25 foot putt for his par. Having marked the position of his ball he lifted it and passed to his caddie for cleaning. When it was Langer's turn to putt he bent down to replace his ball but prior to doing so, for some inexplicable reason, he picked up his marker, at which point he stood up with both marker and ball in his hand. Having been penalised one stroke under Rule 20-1 Langer replaced his marker as near as possible to its original position, replaced the ball and proceeded to take three putts and lose the Tournament by two strokes.

RULE **21**

See **incident** involving Rule 21 below

CLEANING BALL

A ball on the *putting green* may be cleaned when lifted under Rule l6-1b. Elsewhere, a ball may be cleaned when lifted except when it has been lifted:
a. To determine if it is unfit for play (Rule 5-3);
b. For identification (Rule 12-2), in which case it may be cleaned only to the extent necessary for identification; or
c. Because it is interfering with or assisting play (Rule 22).

If a player cleans his ball during play of a hole except as provided in this Rule, **he shall incur a penalty of one stroke** and the ball, if lifted, shall be replaced.

If a player who is required to replace a ball fails to do so, **he shall incur the penalty** for breach of Rule 20-3a, but no additional penalty under Rule 21 shall be applied.

Exception: If a player incurs a penalty for failing to act in accordance with Rule 5-3, 12-2 or 22, no additional penalty under Rule 21 shall be applied.

RULE 21 INCIDENT

During the 1999 U.S. Open at Pinehurst – six holes after the incident described under Rule 22 (see page 86) – Scott Hoch holed his bunker shot at the par-4 12th. During the clamour, the walking Rules official looked up to see two senior Rules officials motioning him to come over.

The senior officials reported that a spectator had alleged that Hoch's ball was mistakenly cleaned when lifted for interference at the 6th hole. Rule 22 permits the lifting of a ball that interferes with or assists the play of another player but under such circumstances, except on the putting green, the ball may not be cleaned when lifted under Rule 22.

The senior officials asked the walking official if he could confirm whether Hoch's ball had been cleaned when lifted from the greenside rough. The walking official stated that his attention had been primarily focused on the lifting and replacing procedures and he was unaware of any cleaning breach.

It was decided to ask Hoch about the incident after he finished the round but before he returned his score card. When the inquiry was made Hoch replied that he did not recall since the incident had occurred two hours before. Hoch's caddie also said he did not recall. Parnevik and Jones said they were not watching and could not say.

Since there was no evidence to the contrary, Hoch was found to have acted properly and he began the second round just four shots off the lead.

RULE **22**

See **incident** involving Rule 22 on page 86

BALL INTERFERING WITH OR ASSISTING PLAY

Any player may:

a. Lift his ball if he considers that the ball might assist any other player or

b. Have any other ball lifted if he considers that the ball might interfere with his play or assist the play of any other player, but this may not be done

BALL INTERFERING WITH OR ASSISTING PLAY

As we're playing a match, I would like you to leave your ball where it is.

I'm sorry, but I'm entitled to mark and lift my ball and I'm going to do so.

while another ball is in motion. In stroke play, a player required to lift his ball may play first rather than lift. A ball lifted under this Rule shall be replaced.

PENALTY FOR BREACH OF RULE:
Match play — Loss of hole; Stroke play — Two strokes.
Note: Except on the *putting green*, the ball may not be cleaned when lifted under this Rule — see Rule 21.

RULE 22 INCIDENT

Because golf is played on the largest playing field of any sport, it's rare for one ball to touch another.

However, Jesper Parnevik and Scott Hoch found themselves in such a predicament just off the 6th green at Pinehurst No.2 during the 1999 U.S. Open. Fortunately, the procedure in such a situation is concise.

The shortest Rule in the book, Rule 22 allows any player to lift his ball if he believes it will assist another player, or have any ball lifted that might interfere with his play or assist any other player. Except on the putting green, a ball lifted under this Rule may not be cleaned.

Hoch and Parnevik both played just to the left side of the green at this 222-yard par 3. Upon arriving at the green, they found that the balls were touching one another and lay about three inches off the fringe in the Bermuda grass rough. Both balls were held slightly off the ground by the stiff nature of the grass. Because Hoch's ball was closer to the hole, it was necessary that it be lifted in order for Parnevik to play his shot.

When Hoch lifted his ball, Parnevik's moved an inch closer to the hole. Under a Rules official's watchful eye, Parnevik attempted to replace his ball in its original location. However, the supporting nature of the Bermuda grass could not be reintroduced and Parnevik's ball sunk a littler deeper into the rough than its original position. Under the Rules, it doesn't matter if the movement is vertical or horizontal. The ball could not be replaced in its original position so that it would remain at rest.

Rule 20-3d covers such a situation by stating that if a ball, when placed or replaced, fails to come to rest on that spot it shall be replaced. If it again fails to remain at rest, it must be placed at the nearest spot where it can be placed at rest which is not nearer the hole and not in a hazard.

Therefore, Parnevik found another spot that was nearest to the original position where the ball would remain at rest. He chipped onto the green and in doing so altered Hoch's lie.

In this case, Hoch was entitled to the lie that his shot gave him. Since his lie had been altered, he found the nearest lie most similar to and within one club-length of his original lie placed his ball at that spot. Then he chipped in for a birdie two.

All of this was under the discerning eyes of both the walking Rules official and a Rules rover who was monitoring the group's pace of play. Parnevik and Jones finished the hole and the group went to the 7th tee. See Rule 21 for a continuation of this incident.

A player is entitled to remove any loose impediment without penalty, except when both the loose impediment and the player's ball lie in or touch the same hazard.

RULE **23** | # LOOSE IMPEDIMENTS

DEFINITIONS

Loose impediments are natural objects such as stones, leaves, twigs, branches and the like, dung, worms and insects and casts or heaps made by them, provided they are not fixed or growing, are not solidly embedded and do not adhere to the ball.

Sand and loose soil are loose impediments on the *putting green* but not elsewhere.

Snow and natural ice, other than frost, are either *casual water* or loose impediments, at the option of the player. Manufactured ice is an *obstruction*.

Dew and frost are not loose impediments.

Loose impediments are natural objects that come in all shapes and sizes. At the 1999 Phoenix Open, Tiger Woods learned that a player can receive assistance in removing a large loose impediment. Details of this incident can be reviewed on page 88.

See **incident** involving Rule 23-1 below

23-1 RELIEF

Except when both the *loose impediment* and the ball lie in or touch the same *hazard*, any loose impediment may be removed without penalty. If the ball *moves*, see Rule 18-2c.

When a ball is in motion, a *loose impediment* which might influence the movement of the ball shall not be removed.

PENALTY FOR BREACH OF RULE:

Match play — Loss of hole; Stroke play — Two strokes.

(Searching for ball in hazard — see Rule 12-1.)

(Touching line of putt — see Rule 16-1a.)

RULE 23 INCIDENT

The Rules of Golf permitted Tiger Woods to gain assistance from his substantial gallery in moving a loose impediment during the 1999 Phoenix Open.

During the final round, Woods' drive from the 13th tee travelled 360 yards before finishing in the desert just off the left side of the fairway. The ball stopped about two feet directly behind a boulder that was roughly four feet wide, two feet high and two feet thick. The rock was too heavy for Woods to move by himself, and his ball was too close to it to play over or around. Without moving the rock, his best option would have been to play sideways into the fairway.

With 225 yards to the putting green, Woods was not inclined to pitch out without first knowing what his options were with regard to the rock.

A PGA Tour Rules official appeared at the scene. With a glimmer of a smile on his face, Woods kicked the rock and asked, "... It's not a pebble but is it a loose impediment?"

The definition within the Rules of Golf states that loose impediments are natural objects that are not fixed or growing, not solidly embedded and do not adhere to the ball. There is no reference to size or weight.

Decision 23-1/2 states that stones of any size are loose impediments and may be removed, as long as they are not solidly embedded and their removal does not unduly delay play.

The official replied, "It's readily movable if you have people who can move it real quick."

"Really?" Woods responded to the revelation quietly.

Then the official added in an inquiring tone, "But it kind of looks embedded to me."

"It's embedded?" Woods asked as they both stepped back to look.

The official decided the stone was just lying on the desert floor and was not solidly embedded. He also knew that Decision 23-1/3 specifically permits spectators, caddies, fellow-competitors, essentially anyone to assist in removing a large loose impediment.

Several men rolled the stone out of Woods' line of play as others watched and cheered. Following the removal, Woods shook each man's hand and then played his shot directly toward the green, where it finished in the bunker to the right of the green.

RULE **24** OBSTRUCTIONS

DEFINITIONS

The **nearest point of relief** is the reference point for taking relief without penalty from interference by an immovable *obstruction* (Rule 24-2), an *abnormal ground condition* (Rule 25-1) or a *wrong putting green* (see Rule 25-3).

It is the point on the *course*, nearest to where the ball lies, which is not nearer the hole and at which, if the ball were so positioned, no interference (as defined) would exist.

Note: The player should determine his nearest point of relief by using the club with which he expects to play his next stroke to simulate the address position and swing for such stroke.

An **obstruction** is anything artificial, including the artificial surfaces and sides of roads and paths and manufactured ice, except:

a. Objects defining *out of bounds*, such as walls, fences, stakes and railings;

b. Any part of an immovable artificial object which is *out of bounds*; and

c. Any construction declared by the *Committee* to be an integral part of the course.

An obstruction is a movable obstruction if it may be moved without unreasonable effort, without unduly delaying play and without causing damage. Otherwise, it is an immovable obstruction.

Note: The *Committee* may make a Local Rule declaring a movable obstruction to be an immovable obstruction.

BALL AGAINST RAKE ROLLS INTO BUNKER WHEN RAKE REMOVED

See **incident**
involving Rule 24-1
on page 95

24-1 MOVABLE OBSTRUCTION

A player may obtain relief from a movable *obstruction* as follows:

a. If the ball does not lie in or on the *obstruction*, the obstruction may be removed. If the ball *moves*, it shall be replaced, and there is no penalty provided that the movement of the ball is directly attributable to the removal of the obstruction. Otherwise, Rule 18-2a applies.

b. If the ball lies in or on the *obstruction*, the ball may be lifted, without penalty, and the obstruction removed. The ball shall *through the green* or in a *hazard* be dropped, or on the *putting green* be placed, as near as possible to the spot directly under the place where the ball lay in or on the obstruction, but not nearer the hole.

The ball may be cleaned when lifted under Rule 24-1.

When a ball is in motion, an obstruction which might influence the movement of the ball, other than an attended *flagstick* or *equipment* of the players, shall not be removed.

(Exerting influence on the ball — see Rule 1-2.)

Note: If a ball to be dropped or placed under this Rule is not immediately recoverable, another ball may be substituted.

24-2 IMMOVABLE OBSTRUCTION
a Interference

Interference by an immovable *obstruction* occurs when a ball lies in or on the obstruction, or so close to the obstruction that the obstruction interferes with the player's *stance* or the area of his intended swing. If the player's ball lies on the *putting green*, interference also occurs if an immovable obstruction on the putting green intervenes on his *line of putt*. Otherwise, intervention on the *line of play* is not, of itself, interference under this Rule.

b Relief

See **incidents**
involving Rule 24-2b
on page 95

Except when the ball is in a *water hazard* or a *lateral water hazard*, a player may obtain relief from interference by an immovable *obstruction*, without penalty, as follows:

(i)   **Through the Green**: If the ball lies *through the green*, the *nearest point of relief* shall be determined which is not in a *hazard* or on a *putting green*. The player shall lift the ball and drop it within one club-length of and not nearer the hole than the nearest point of relief, on a part of the *course* which avoids interference (as defined) by the immovable *obstruction* and is not in a hazard or on a putting green.

(ii) **In a Bunker:** If the ball is in a *bunker*, the player shall lift and drop the ball in accordance with Clause (i) above, except that the *nearest point of relief* must be in the bunker and the ball must be dropped in the bunker.

(iii) **On the Putting Green:** If the ball lies on the *putting green*, the player shall lift the ball and place it at the *nearest point of relief* which is not in a *hazard*. The nearest point of relief may be off the putting green.

RELIEF FROM OBSTRUCTION GIVES RELIEF FOR LINE OF PLAY

The ball may be cleaned when lifted under Rule 24-2b.
(Ball rolling to a position where there is interference by the condition from which relief was taken — see Rule 20-2c(v).)
Exception: A player may not obtain relief under Rule 24–2b if (a) it is clearly unreasonable for him to play a stroke because of interference by anything other than an immovable *obstruction* or (b) interference by an immovable obstruction would occur only through use of an unnecessarily abnormal *stance*, swing or direction of play.

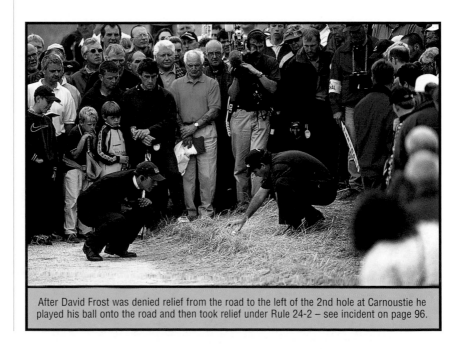

After David Frost was denied relief from the road to the left of the 2nd hole at Carnoustie he played his ball onto the road and then took relief under Rule 24-2 – see incident on page 96.

NO RELIEF WITHOUT PENALTY IN WATER HAZARD

Although my ball is in the hazard it is playable, except that pipe interferes with my swing. May I take free relief?

I'm afraid not. Your ball is in a water hazard and there is no free relief from an immovable obstruction in this situation. You will have to play it or proceed under the Water Hazard Rule.

BALL ON BRIDGE ABOVE HAZARD

The ball is in the water hazard because the margins of a water hazard are deemed to extend vertically upwards. The bridge is an immovable obstruction but there is no relief without penalty from an immovable obstruction when the ball lies in or touches a water hazard. If the ball is played from the bridge the club may be grounded.

STILE IN BOUNDARY FENCE

The stile interferes with my follow-through. May I obtain free relief?

Yes. The out of bounds fence is not an immovable obstruction, but the stile is.

Note 1: If a ball is in a *water hazard* (including a *lateral water hazard*), the player is not entitled to relief without penalty from interference by an immovable *obstruction*. The player shall play the ball as it lies or proceed under Rule 26-1.

Note 2: If a ball to be dropped or placed under this Rule is not immediately recoverable, another ball may be substituted.

Note 3: The *Committee* may make a Local Rule stating that the player must determine the *nearest point of relief* without crossing over, through or under the *obstruction*.

c Ball lost

It is a question of fact whether a ball lost after having been struck toward an immovable *obstruction* is lost in the obstruction. In order to treat the ball as lost in the obstruction, there must be reasonable evidence to that effect. In the absence of such evidence, the ball must be treated as a *lost ball* and Rule 27 applies.

If a ball is lost in an immovable obstruction, the spot where the ball last entered the obstruction shall be determined and, for the purpose of applying this Rule, the ball shall be deemed to lie at this spot.

(i) **Through the Green:** If the ball last entered the immovable *obstruction* at a spot *through the green*, the player may substitute another ball without penalty and take relief as prescribed in Rule 24-2b(i).

(ii) **In a Bunker:** If the ball last entered the immovable *obstruction* at a spot in a *bunker*, the player may substitute another ball without penalty and take relief as prescribed in Rule 24-2b(ii).

(iii) **In a Water Hazard (including a Lateral Water Hazard):** If the ball last entered the immovable *obstruction* at a spot in a *water hazard*, the player is not entitled to relief without penalty. The player shall proceed under Rule 26-1.

(iv) **On the Putting Green**: If the ball last entered the immovable *obstruction* at a spot on the *putting green*, the player may substitute another ball without penalty and take relief as prescribed in Rule 24-2b(iii).

PENALTY FOR BREACH OF RULE:
Match play — Loss of hole; Stroke play — Two strokes.

RULE 24 INCIDENTS

Since 1744, the basic tenets of the Rules have been to play the course as you find it, the ball as it lies and, if you are unsure of the proper procedure, to do what is fair. Harry Bradshaw held true to this spirit at the 1949 British Open.

Having shot a stunning first round 68 over Royal St. George's Bradshaw was tied with Roberto De Vicenzo one stroke behind Jimmy Adams. However, playing the 5th hole during the second round, Bradshaw's ball rolled into a discarded beer bottle from which the neck had been broken.

Rather than requesting a ruling for the relief to which he was entitled, Bradshaw determined on his own that he must play the ball as it lay. He took out his sand wedge and made a swing, which shattered the bottle and moved the ball slightly forward. He took a double bogey six.

The result of his playing out of this movable obstruction was that Bradshaw ultimately tied Bobby Locke of South Africa at 283. In the resulting 36-hole play-off, Locke scored 136 to Bradshaw's 147, to win the first of Locke's four Open Championships.

Under Rule 24-1, because Bradshaw's ball was in a movable obstruction, the ball could have been lifted and cleaned without penalty, the bottle removed and the ball dropped as nearly as possible to the spot directly under the place where the ball lay when it was in the bottle.

In choosing to take relief from an immovable obstruction, the ball must be dropped in a place that avoids interference by the immovable obstruction. Full relief must be taken. Payne Stewart learned this lesson in 1993 during the PGA Tour's annual stop in San Diego.

In taking relief from a cart path, Stewart dropped his ball in a place where, after taking his stance, the heel of his right shoe was still on the cart path from which he was taking relief. The television broadcast showed the breach clearly and Stewart was penalised two strokes for not taking complete relief from the immovable obstruction.

The Exception to Rule 24-2 states clearly that a player may not obtain relief under this Rule if interference would only occur through the use of an abnormal stance, swing or direction of play. This is one of the places in the Rules where a Referee's judgment is called upon, as David Frost learned during the final round of the 1999 Open Championship at Carnoustie.

Playing with Justin Leonard in the penultimate group, Frost's drive at the second hole was a low hook into the high rough. Near the area where he would stand to play the ball was a road. Frost argued to the attending Rules official that in order to play the ball, which was below his feet, he would have to widen his stance to such an extent that he would be standing on the road and, therefore, he was entitled to relief from an immovable obstruction.

The referee did not accept the argument and told Frost that such a play was not reasonable. It was the official's judgment that had the road not been there, Frost would not have used a stance that would place his left foot on the road. With the final pairing waiting on the tee, time ticked away as confirmation of the official's decision was requested over the radio. It was deemed final, and Frost played the ball as it lay. His shot from this awkward lie came to rest on the road, from where he was then granted relief under Rule 24-2.

In such a situation, the Rules official must consider how the player would attempt the shot if the obstruction in question were not present. In a stroke play situation such as this one, the Rules are there to protect the field and prevent an unfair advantage of one player over all the others.

When the Committee declares an obstruction an integral part of the golf course, it eliminates any argument because there is no free

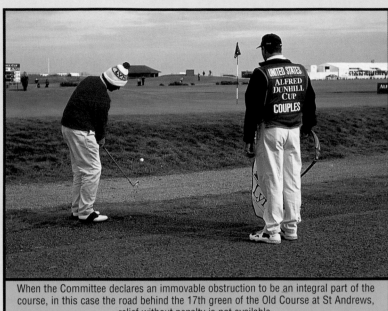

When the Committee declares an immovable obstruction to be an integral part of the course, in this case the road behind the 17th green of the Old Course at St Andrews, relief without penalty is not available.

relief. The most famous example of this is on the Road Hole at the Old Course in St Andrews. When a ball lies on the road immediately to the right of the green, it must be played as it lies. As the name of the hole suggests, the road has always been the most important element of the 17th hole, and to allow relief would eliminate one of its essential obstacles. Thus, it is an integral part of the golf course.

RULE 25 ABNORMAL GROUND CONDITIONS, EMBEDDED BALL AND WRONG PUTTING GREEN

DEFINITIONS

An **abnormal ground condition** is any *casual water*, *ground under repair* or a hole, cast or runway on the *course* made by a *burrowing animal*, a reptile or a bird.

A **burrowing animal** is an animal that makes a hole for habitation or shelter, such as a rabbit, mole, groung hog, gopher or salamander. **Note:** A hole made by a non-burrowing animal, such as a dog, is not an *abnormal ground condition* unless marked or declared as *ground under repair*.

Casual water is any temporary accumulation of water on the *course* which is visible before or after the player takes his *stance* and is not in a *water hazard*. Snow and natural ice, other than frost, are casual water or *loose impediments*, at the option of the player. Manufactured ice is an *obstruction*. Dew and frost are not casual water. A ball is in casual water when it lies in or any part of it touches the casual water.

97

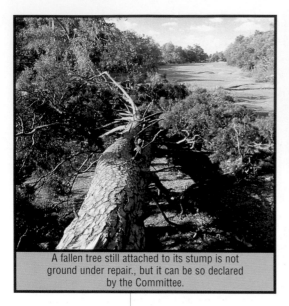

A fallen tree still attached to its stump is not ground under repair., but it can be so declared by the Committee.

A rut made by a tractor is not ground under repair, but the Committee would be justified in declaring a deep rut to be ground under repair.

Ground under repair is any part of the *course* so marked by order of the *Committee* or so declared by its authorised representative. It includes material piled for removal and a hole made by a greenkeeper, even if not so marked.

All ground and any grass, bush, tree or other growing thing within the ground under repair is part of the ground under repair. The margin of ground under repair extends vertically downwards, but not upwards. Stakes and lines defining ground under repair are in such ground. Such stakes are *obstructions*. A ball is in ground under repair when it lies in or any part of it touches the ground under repair.

AREAS REQUIRING PRESERVATION

If there is an area of the course, such as a plantation of young trees, which requires preservation the Committee should declare it "Ground Under Repair – Play Prohibited".

Note 1: Grass cuttings and other material left on the *course* which have been abandoned and are not intended to be removed are not ground under repair unless so marked.

Note 2: The *Committee* may make a Local Rule prohibiting play from ground under repair or an environmentally-sensitive area which has been defined as ground under repair.

The **nearest point of relief** is the reference point for taking relief without penalty from interference by an immovable *obstruction* (Rule 24-2), an *abnormal ground condition* (Rule 25-1) or a *wrong putting green* (Rule 25-3).

It is the point on the *course*, nearest to where the ball lies, which is not nearer the hole and at which, if the ball were so positioned, no interference (as defined) would exist.

Note: The player should determine his nearest point of relief by using the club with which he expects to play his next stroke to simulate the address position and swing for such stroke.

A **wrong putting green** is any *putting green* other than that of the hole being played. Unless otherwise prescribed by the *Committee*, this term includes a practice putting green or pitching green on the *course*.

25-1 ABNORMAL GROUND CONDITIONS

a Interference

Interference by an *abnormal ground condition* occurs when a ball lies in or touches the condition or when such a condition interferes with the player's *stance* or the area of his intended swing. If the player's ball lies on the *putting green*, interference also occurs if such condition on the putting green intervenes on his *line of putt*. Otherwise, intervention on the *line of play* is not, of itself, interference under this Rule.

Note: The *Committee* may make a Local Rule denying the player relief from interference with his *stance* by an *abnormal ground condition*.

See **incident** involving Rule 25-1b on page 104

b Relief

Except when the ball is in a *water hazard* or a *lateral water hazard*, a player may obtain relief from interference by an *abnormal ground condition* as follows:

(i) **Through the Green:** If the ball lies *through the green*, the *nearest point of relief* shall be determined which is not in a *hazard* or on a *putting green*. The player shall lift the ball and drop it without penalty within one club-length of and not nearer the hole than the nearest point of relief, on a part of the *course* which avoids interference (as defined) by the condition and is not in a hazard or on a putting green.

(ii) **In a Bunker:** If the ball is in a *bunker*, the player shall lift and drop the ball either:
(a) Without penalty, in accordance with Clause (i) above, except that the *nearest point of relief* must be in the bunker and the ball must be dropped in the bunker, or if complete relief is impossible, in the bunker as near as possible to the spot where the ball lay, but not nearer the hole, on a part of the *course* which affords maximum available relief from the condition; or

99

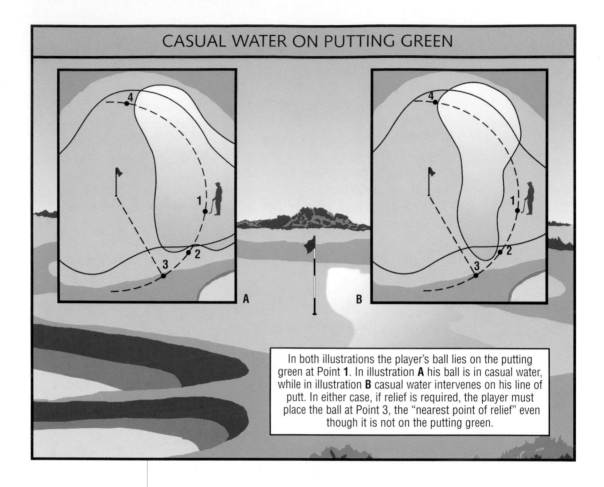

CASUAL WATER ON PUTTING GREEN

In both illustrations the player's ball lies on the putting green at Point **1**. In illustration **A** his ball is in casual water, while in illustration **B** casual water intervenes on his line of putt. In either case, if relief is required, the player must place the ball at Point **3**, the "nearest point of relief" even though it is not on the putting green.

    (b) **Under penalty of one stroke**, outside the bunker keeping the point where the ball lay directly between the hole and the spot on which the ball is dropped, with no limit to how far behind the bunker the ball may be dropped.

(iii) **On the Putting Green:** If the ball lies on the *putting green*, the player shall lift the ball and place it without penalty at the *nearest point of relief* which is not in a *hazard*, or if complete relief is impossible, at the nearest position to where it lay which affords maximum available relief from the condition, but not nearer the hole nor in a hazard. The nearest point of relief or maximum available relief may be off the putting green.

The ball may be cleaned when lifted under Rule 25-1b.

(Ball rolling to a position where there is interference by the condition from which relief was taken – see Rule 20-2c(v).)

Exception: A player may not obtain relief under Rule 25-1b if (a) it is clearly unreasonable for him to play a stroke because of interference by anything other than an *abnormal ground condition* or (b) interference by such a condition would occur only through use of an unnecessarily abnormal *stance*, swing or direction of play.

Note 1: If a ball is in a *water hazard* (including a *lateral water hazard*), the player is not entitled to relief without penalty from interference by an *abnormal ground condition*. The player shall play the ball as it lies (unless prohibited by Local Rule) or proceed under Rule 26-1.

Note 2: If a ball to be dropped or placed under this Rule is not immediately recoverable, another ball may be substituted.

c Ball Lost

See **incident** involving Rule 25-1c on page 105

It is a question of fact whether a ball lost after having been struck toward an *abnormal ground condition* is lost in such condition. In order to treat the ball as lost in the abnormal ground condition, there must be reasonable evidence to that effect. In the absence of such evidence, the ball must be treated as a *lost ball* and Rule 27 applies.

If a ball is lost in an abnormal ground condition, the spot where the ball last entered the condition shall be determined and, for the purposes of applying this Rule, the ball shall be deemed to lie at this spot.

(i) **Through the Green:** If the ball last entered the *abnormal ground condition* at a spot *through the green*, the player may substitute another ball without penalty and take relief as prescribed in Rule 25-1b(i).

(ii) **In a Bunker:** If the ball last entered the *abnormal ground condition* at a spot in a *bunker*, the player may substitute another ball without penalty and take relief as prescribed in Rule 25-1b(ii).

(iii) **In a Water Hazard (including a Lateral Water Hazard):** If the ball last entered the *abnormal ground condition* at a spot in a *water hazard*, the player is not entitled to relief without penalty. The player shall proceed under Rule 26-1.

(iv) **On the Putting Green:** If the ball last entered the *abnormal ground condition* at a spot on the *putting green*, the player may substitute another ball without penalty and take relief as prescribed in Rule 25-1b(iii).

BALL CLOSE TO CASUAL WATER: LEFT HANDED STROKE NOT REASONABLE

25-2 EMBEDDED BALL

A ball embedded in its own pitch-mark in the ground in any closely-mown area *through the green* may be lifted, cleaned and dropped, without penalty, as near as possible to the spot where it lay but not nearer the hole. The ball when dropped must first strike a part of the *course* through the green.

"Closely-mown area" means any area of the course, including paths through the rough, cut to fairway height or less.

25-3 WRONG PUTTING GREEN

a Interference

Interference by a *wrong putting green* occurs when a ball is on the wrong putting green.

Interference to a player's *stance* or the area of his intended swing is not, of itself, interference under this Rule.

b Relief

If a player has interference by a *wrong putting green*, the player must take relief, without penalty, as follows:

The *nearest point of relief* shall be determined which is not in a *hazard* or on a *putting green*. The player shall lift the ball and drop it within one club-length of and not nearer the hole than the nearest point of relief, on a part of the *course* which avoids interference (as defined) by the wrong putting green and is not in a hazard or on a putting green. The ball may be cleaned when so lifted.

PENALTY FOR BREACH OF RULE:

Match play — Loss of hole; Stroke play — Two strokes.

RULE 25 INCIDENTS

Tied for the lead going into the final hole of the 1994 Volvo Masters at Valderrama, Severiano Ballesteros pushed his tee shot right and the ball came to rest at the base of a tree, close to a large hole.

The tree was positioned directly between the ball and the hole and Ballesteros, having examined the lie of the ball, decided to call for a

Rules official. Ballesteros felt that his ball was lying in earth which had been removed by whatever had dug the hole and, therefore, he thought he may be entitled to free relief from the condition under Rule 25-1. However, as the Rules official was to explain to him, free relief would only be available if the hole had been made by a burrowing animal and the hole or cast was deemed to interfere with the lie of his ball or the area of his intended swing. The official undertook a thorough search for evidence that the hole had been made by a burrowing animal but could find no such evidence and thus denied Ballesteros relief.

The referee's decision was crucial in that if Ballesteros had been entitled to the relief he requested it was apparent that he would have been able to drop a ball in accordance with the Rules, in a position where the tree would no longer have interfered with his line of play and he would have had a clear shot to the green. It transpired that with the relief denied Ballesteros had to chip out sideways and his chance of victory was gone.

During the second round of The Players Championship in 1999, marshals at the 18th green watched Greg Norman's ball roll into a hole made by a burrowing animal. When a ball is lost in an abnormal ground condition, there must be reasonable evidence to that effect. Suspecting that the ball might have gone into the burrowing animal hole is not good enough and, indeed, the Australian started to put his hand into the hole to determine if the ball was there.

The attending official told Norman that the marshals' statements that they had seen the ball go into the burrowing animal hole constituted reasonable evidence. Therefore, he was entitled to relief without penalty, and it was not necessary to reach into the hole in order to retrieve the ball.

"A hole or cast made by a non-burrowing animal is not an abnormal ground condition". Seve Ballesteros is denied relief under Rule 25-1 on the final hole of the 1994 Volvo Masters.

RULE 26 | WATER HAZARDS (INCLUDING LATERAL WATER HAZARDS)

DEFINITIONS

A **water hazard** is any sea, lake, pond, river, ditch, surface drainage ditch or other open water course (whether or not containing water) and anything of a similar nature.

All ground or water within the margin of a water hazard is part of the water hazard. The margin of a water hazard extends vertically upwards and downwards. Stakes and lines defining the margins of water hazards are in the hazards. Such stakes are *obstructions*. A ball is in a water hazard when it lies in or any part of it touches the water hazard.

Note 1: Water hazards (other than *lateral water hazards*) should be defined by yellow stakes or lines.

Note 2: The *Committee* may make a Local Rule prohibiting play from an environmentally-sensitive area which has been defined as a water hazard.

A **lateral water hazard** is a *water hazard* or that part of a water hazard so situated that it is not possible or is deemed by the *Committee* to be impracticable to drop a ball behind the water hazard in accordance with Rule 26-1b.

That part of a water hazard to be played as a lateral water hazard should be distinctively marked. A ball is in a lateral water hazard when it lies in or any part of it touches the lateral water hazard.

Note 1: Lateral water hazards should be defined by red stakes or lines.

Note 2: The *Committee* may make a Local Rule prohibiting play from an environmentally-sensitive area which has been defined as a lateral water hazard.

Note 3: The *Committee* may define a lateral water hazard as a water hazard.

26-1 BALL IN WATER HAZARD

It is a question of fact whether a ball lost after having been struck toward a *water hazard* is lost inside or outside the hazard. In order to treat the ball as lost in the hazard, there must be reasonable evidence that the ball

Jean Van de Velde's difficulty with the Barry Burn at the 72nd hole of the 1999 British Open resulted in a three-way playoff for the championship. See the details of his unfortunate brush with Rule 26-1 in the incident on page 110.

REASONABLE EVIDENCE BALL IN WATER HAZARD

lodged in it. In the absence of such evidence, the ball must be treated as a *lost ball* and Rule 27 applies.

If a ball is in or is lost in a water hazard (whether the ball lies in water or not), the player may **under penalty of one stroke:**

a. Play a ball as nearly as possible at the spot from which the original ball was last played (see Rule 20-5); or

b. Drop a ball behind the water hazard, keeping the point at which the original ball last crossed the margin of the water hazard directly between the hole and the spot on which the ball is dropped, with no limit to how far behind the water hazard the ball may be dropped; or

c. As additional options available only if the ball last crossed the margin of a lateral water hazard, drop a ball outside the water hazard within two club-lengths of and not nearer the hole than (i) the point where the original ball last crossed the margin of the water hazard or (ii) a point on the opposite margin of the water hazard equidistant from the hole.

The ball may be cleaned when lifted under this Rule.

(Ball moving in water in a water hazard — see Rule 14-6.)

See incident involving Rule 26-1b on page 110

26-2 BALL PLAYED WITHIN WATER HAZARD
a Ball Comes to Rest in the Hazard

If a ball played from within a *water hazard* comes to rest in the same hazard after the *stroke*, the player may:

(i) proceed under Rule 26-1; or

(ii) **under penalty of one stroke**, play a ball as nearly as possible at the spot from which the last stroke from outside the hazard was played (see Rule 20-5).

107

BALL CROSSING MARGIN OF WATER HAZARD

My ball crossed the water hazard, but spun back into it. Where do I take relief?

Under penalty of one stroke, you may play a ball from where you last played, or you may drop a ball behind the hazard on an extension of the line from the hole to the point at which the ball last crossed the margin (point **B**). The point at which the ball first crossed the margin (Point **A**) is irrelevant.

RELIEF FROM LATERAL WATER HAZARD

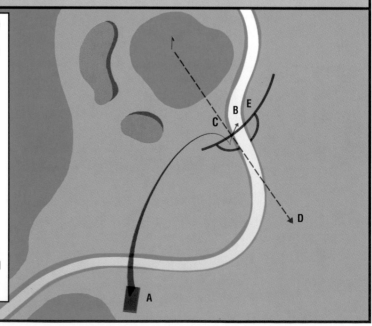

The player has played a ball from the tee (Point **A**) into the lateral water hazard at Point **B.** It last crossed the margin of the hazard at Point **C** and the point on the opposite margin, equidistant from the hole is Point **E**. He may play the ball as it lies or, under penalty of one stroke;
(i) play another ball from the tee - Rule 26-1a;
(ii) drop a ball anywhere on the far side of the hazard on the dotted line from the hole through Point **C**, e.g. Point **D** - Rule 26-1b;
(iii) drop a ball in the area on the near side of the hazard which is all ground within two club-lengths of Point **C** - Rule 26-1c(i); or
(iv) drop a ball in the area on the far side of the hazard which is all ground within two club-lengths of Point **E** - Rule 26-1c(ii).

BALL PLAYED FROM WITHIN WATER HAZARD

The player's tee shot at a par 3 hole comes to rest in a water hazard. He plays from the hazard, but fails to get his ball out. He may play the ball as it lies or, under penalty of one stroke:
(i) drop a ball at the spot from which he's just played his second stroke and play again from there;
(ii) drop a ball behind the hazard, anywhere on the dotted line, and play from there; or
(iii) play another ball from the tee.

If the player proceeds under Rule 26-1a, he may elect not to play the dropped ball. If he so elects, he may:

a. Proceed under Rule 26-1b, **adding the additional penalty of one stroke** prescribed by that Rule; or

b. Proceed under Rule 26-1c, if applicable, **adding the additional penalty of one stroke** prescribed by that Rule; or

c. **Add an additional penalty of one stroke** and play a ball as nearly as possible at the spot from which the last stroke from outside the hazard was played (see Rule 20-5).

b Ball Lost or Unplayable Outside Hazard or Out of Bounds

If a ball played from within a *water hazard* is lost or declared unplayable outside the hazard or is *out of bounds*, the player, after taking **a penalty of one stroke** under Rule 27-1 or 28a, may:

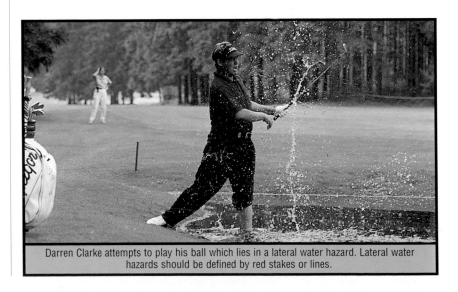

Darren Clarke attempts to play his ball which lies in a lateral water hazard. Lateral water hazards should be defined by red stakes or lines.

(i)   play a ball as nearly as possible at the spot in the hazard from which the original ball was last played (see Rule 20-5); or

(ii)   proceed under Rule 26-1b, or if applicable Rule 26-1c, **adding the additional penalty of one stroke** prescribed by the Rule and using as the reference point the point where the original ball last crossed the margin of the hazard before it came to rest in the hazard; or

(iii)   **add an additional penalty of one stroke** and play a ball as nearly as possible at the spot from which the last stroke from outside the hazard was played (see Rule 20-5).

Note 1: When proceeding under Rule 26-2b, the player is not required to drop a ball under Rule 27-1 or 28a. If he does drop a ball, he is not required to play it. He may alternatively proceed under Clause (ii) or (iii).

Note 2: If a ball played from within a water hazard is declared unplayable outside the hazard, nothing in Rule 26-2b precludes the player from proceeding under Rule 28b or c.

PENALTY FOR BREACH OF RULE:

Match play — Loss of hole; Stroke play — Two strokes.

RULE 26 INCIDENT

Standing on Carnoustie's 18th tee, in the final round of the 1999 Open Championship, Jean Van de Velde needed only a double bogey to become the first Frenchman to win the championship since 1907.

Minutes later, with his navy blue trousers rolled to his knees, he was standing in the Barry Burn contemplating his fate and his options under Rule 26.

Having played a driver from the tee, the Frenchman's ball had finished well right but safely on a peninsula created by a bend in the burn. Instead of laying up with his second, Van de Velde attempted to play a 2-iron to the distant green. His shot was a bit wayward and it ricocheted off a grandstand railing, the stone wall of the water hazard and finally settled behind the second crossing of the burn in heavy rough.

Attempting to hit his ball out of the rough and over the burn, he played it badly and the ball finished in the shallow water of the burn. As the stream runs perpendicular to the line of play, it was marked with a yellow line indicating a water hazard.

As such, Van de Velde had three options. He could play the ball without penalty as it lay. Under penalty of one stroke, he could play again from where he last played, or he could drop behind the hazard keeping the point at which his ball last crossed the margin of the water hazard directly between the hole and the spot on which the ball would be dropped, with no limit to how far behind the hazard he might want to go.

Three in the water, and needing a six to win The Open, the Frenchman contemplated playing out of the hazard in order to avoid the penalty stroke. To make such an assessment, he decided to go into the water to see what the shot required. Having removed his shoes and socks, Van de Velde rolled up his trouser legs and lowered himself down the stone wall into the shallow water.

Van de Velde was left standing alone in the dark water, wedge in hand, assessing his ability to play the submerged ball out of the hazard. After several minutes, discretion became the better part of valour and Van de Velde chose option b under Rule 26-1. He dropped a ball behind the hazard on the stipulated line, suffered a penalty stroke and played his fifth shot to the right greenside bunker. His up-and-down from the bunker resulted in a score of seven and a play-off between himself, Paul Lawrie and Justin Leonard, which Lawrie went on to win.

RULE 27

BALL LOST OR OUT OF BOUNDS; PROVISIONAL BALL

DEFINITIONS

See **incident** involving the Definition of "Lost Ball" on page 114

A ball is **lost** if:

a. It is not found or identified as his by the player within five minutes after the player's *side* or his or their *caddies* have begun to search for it; or

b. The player has put another ball into play under the *Rules*, even though he may not have searched for the original ball; or

c. The player has played any stroke with a *provisional ball* from the place where the original ball is likely to be or from a point nearer the hole than that place, whereupon the provisional ball becomes the *ball in play*.

PLAYERS UNABLE TO IDENTIFY THEIR BALLS

Time spent in playing a *wrong ball* is not counted in the five-minute period allowed for search.

Out of bounds is beyond the boundaries of the *course* or any part of the course so marked by the *Committee*.

When out of bounds is defined by reference to stakes or a fence, or as being beyond stakes or a fence, the out of bounds line is determined by the nearest inside points of the stakes or fence posts at ground level excluding angled supports.

Objects defining out of bounds such as walls, fences, stakes and railings, are not *obstructions* and are deemed to be fixed.

When out of bounds is defined by a line on the ground, the line itself is out of bounds.

The out of bounds line extends vertically upwards and downwards.

A ball is out of bounds when all of it lies out of bounds.

A player may stand out of bounds to play a ball lying within bounds.

A **provisional ball** is a ball played under Rule 27-2 for a ball which may be *lost* outside a *water hazard* or may be *out of bounds*.

27-1 BALL LOST OR OUT OF BOUNDS

If a ball is *lost* or is *out of bounds*, the player shall play a ball, **under penalty of one stroke**, as nearly as possible at the spot from which the original ball was last played (see Rule 20-5).

Exceptions:

1. If there is reasonable evidence that the original ball is lost in a *water hazard*, the player shall proceed in accordance with Rule 26-1.

2. If there is reasonable evidence that the original ball is lost in an immovable *obstruction* (Rule 24-2c) or an *abnormal ground condition* (Rule 25-1c) the player may proceed under the applicable *Rule*.

PENALTY FOR BREACH OF RULE 27-1:

Match play — Loss of hole; Stroke play — Two strokes.

27-2 PROVISIONAL BALL

a Procedure

If a ball may be *lost* outside a *water hazard* or may be *out of bounds*, to save time the player may play another ball provisionally in accordance with Rule 27-1. The player shall inform his opponent in match play or his *marker* or a *fellow-competitor* in stroke play that he intends to play a *provisional ball*, and he shall play it before he or his partner goes forward to search for the original ball.

If he fails to do so and plays another ball, such ball is not a provisional ball and becomes the *ball in play* **under penalty of stroke and distance** (Rule 27-1); the original ball is deemed to be lost.

(Order of play from teeing ground — see Rule 10-3.)

b When Provisional Ball Becomes Ball in Play

The player may play a *provisional ball* until he reaches the place where the original ball is likely to be. If he plays a *stroke* with the provisional ball from the place where the original ball is likely to be or from a point nearer the hole than that place, the original ball is deemed to be *lost* and the provisional ball becomes the *ball in play* **under penalty of stroke and distance** (Rule 27-1).

PROVISIONAL BALL BECOMES BALL IN PLAY

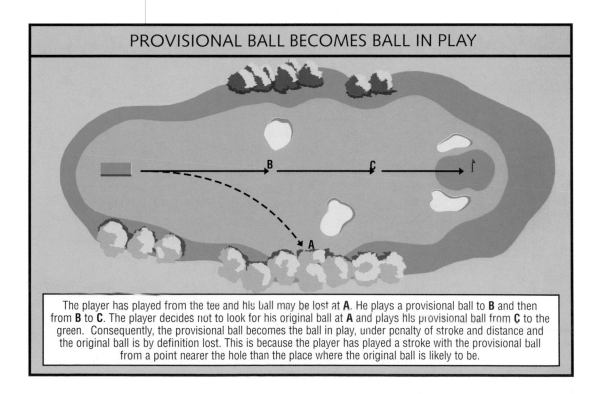

The player has played from the tee and his ball may be lost at **A**. He plays a provisional ball to **B** and then from **B** to **C**. The player decides not to look for his original ball at **A** and plays his provisional ball from **C** to the green. Consequently, the provisional ball becomes the ball in play, under penalty of stroke and distance and the original ball is by definition lost. This is because the player has played a stroke with the provisional ball from a point nearer the hole than the place where the original ball is likely to be.

PROVISIONAL BALL PLAYED: ORIGINAL BALL FOUND UNPLAYABLE

A player plays a provisional ball as his ball may be lost. The original ball is found within five minutes and before the provisional ball has become the ball in play, but the ball is unplayable. The player must abandon the provisional ball and proceed with the original ball.

If the original ball is *lost* outside a *water hazard* or is *out of bounds*, the provisional ball becomes the ball in play, **under penalty of stroke and distance** (Rule 27-1).

If there is reasonable evidence that the original ball is lost in a water hazard, the player shall proceed in accordance with Rule 26-1.

Exception: If there is reasonable evidence that the original ball is lost in an immovable *obstruction* (Rule 24-2c) or an *abnormal ground condition* (Rule 25-1c), the player may proceed under the applicable Rule.

c When Provisional Ball to be Abandoned

If the original ball is neither *lost* nor *out of bounds*, the player shall abandon the *provisional ball* and continue play with the original ball. If he fails to do so, any further *strokes* played with the provisional ball shall constitute playing a *wrong ball* and the provisions of Rule 15 shall apply.

Note: Strokes taken and *penalty strokes* incurred solely in playing a *provisional ball* subsequently abandoned under Rule 27-2c shall be disregarded.

RULE 27 INCIDENT

During the third round of the 1998 Open Championship at Royal Birkdale, Mark O'Meara's second shot drifted too far to the right into knee high grass and gorse at the 480-yard 6th hole and put into motion a series of events that led to the introduction of a clarifying Decision.

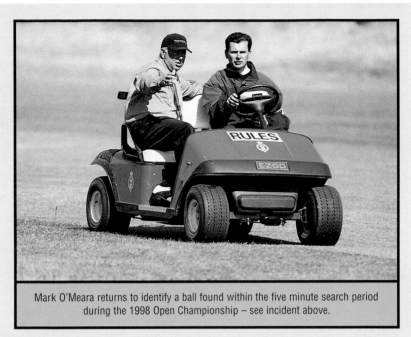

Mark O'Meara returns to identify a ball found within the five minute search period during the 1998 Open Championship – see incident above.

By the time O'Meara and his caddie reached the area where they thought his ball had landed, a number of spectators were already engaged in searching for it. The Rules observer with the group started the clock for the five-minute search period when O'Meara and his caddie arrived.

Several balls were found, but none were O'Meara's. To everyone in the immediate vicinity, he announced the type of ball he was using and stated that it was embossed with his logo.

After searching for approximately four minutes, O'Meara suspected that his ball was lost. He left the search area, took another ball from his caddie, and started back down the fairway to play again from where his original ball had been played.

About 30 seconds later, a spectator announced, "Here it is. I have it." Someone called to O'Meara, who apparently did not hear and continued walking. An official went to where the spectator had found the ball and saw it was the type O'Meara was using and did have his logo on it.

By this time, it was nearing the end of the five-minute search period permitted under the Rules, and it was clear that O'Meara would not be able to get back to the ball in order to identify it within the five-minute period. The Definition of "Lost Ball" states that a ball is lost if it is not "found or identified" within five minutes. If the definition said, "found and identified," the procedure would have been clear. A radio call was made for a roving Rules official to make a decision.

The roving official arrived on the scene and brought O'Meara in a cart back up the fairway where a discussion took place. A further official arrived and it was determined that the ball had been found within the five-minute period, that O'Meara was entitled to identify it outside the stipulated time period and, if it was his ball, he was entitled to play it so everyone returned to the area where the ball had been found.

However, during the search, the search area had been trampled and a misguided spectator, who believed the ball had been abandoned, had lifted it. When O'Meara and the official went to the spot, the ball was not there but the spectator was close by and returned the ball to O'Meara who identified it as his. Although the spectator said he knew "exactly" where the ball had been before he lifted it that turned out to be only an approximation.

Under Rules 18-1 and 20-3c, O'Meara was required to drop as nearly as possible to the spot where the ball had been before being lifted by the spectator. When O'Meara dropped the ball, it rolled more than two club-lengths from the spot where it struck a part of the course thus requiring a re-drop. Upon re-dropping, the ball rolled nearer to the hole and O'Meara, therefore, placed it on the spot where it first struck a part of the course when re-dropped. He then played his shot and continued the round, winning the championship the following day.

The ambiguity of the Definition of "Lost Ball," in this particular situation, necessitated the addition of Decision 27/5.5. The new decision simply clarifies that if a ball is found within five minutes, the player is allowed enough time to reach the area and identify it even though the identification takes place after the five-minute search period has elapsed.

RULE **28** BALL UNPLAYABLE

See **incident** involving Rule 28 on page 118

The player may declare his ball unplayable at any place on the *course* except when the ball is in a *water hazard*. The player is the sole judge as to whether his ball is unplayable.

If the player deems his ball to be unplayable, he shall, **under penalty of one stroke**:

a. Play a ball as nearly as possible at the spot from which the original ball was last played (see Rule 20-5); or

b. Drop a ball within two club-lengths of the spot where the ball lay, but not nearer the hole; or

c. Drop a ball behind the point where the ball lay, keeping that point directly between the hole and the spot on which the ball is dropped, with no limit to how far behind that point the ball may be dropped.

If the unplayable ball is in a *bunker*, the player may proceed under Clause a, b or c. If he elects to proceed under Clause b or c, a ball must be dropped in the bunker.

The ball may be cleaned when lifted under this Rule.

PENALTY FOR BREACH OF RULE:
Match play — Loss of hole; Stroke play — Two strokes.

BALL UNPLAYABLE IN BUNKER: PLAYER'S OPTIONS

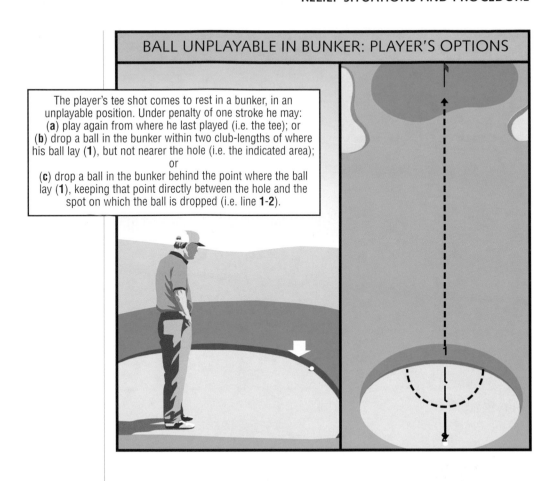

The player's tee shot comes to rest in a bunker, in an unplayable position. Under penalty of one stroke he may:
(**a**) play again from where he last played (i.e. the tee); or
(**b**) drop a ball in the bunker within two club-lengths of where his ball lay (**1**), but not nearer the hole (i.e. the indicated area); or
(**c**) drop a ball in the bunker behind the point where the ball lay (**1**), keeping that point directly between the hole and the spot on which the ball is dropped (i.e. line **1-2**).

BALL UNPLAYABLE IN BUSH: PLACE FOR DROPPING

My ball was in the bush. I've declared it unplayable, and I'm going to invoke option **b** and drop the ball within two club-lengths of where it lay.

That's O.K. But remember the ball when dropped must strike a part of the course within two club-lengths of where it lay.

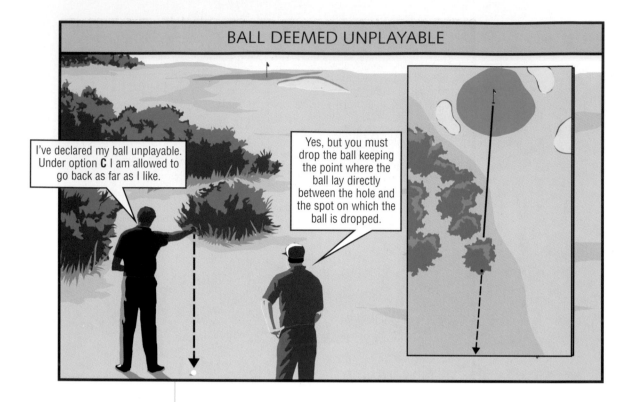

BALL DEEMED UNPLAYABLE

I've declared my ball unplayable. Under option **C** I am allowed to go back as far as I like.

Yes, but you must drop the ball keeping the point where the ball lay directly between the hole and the spot on which the ball is dropped.

RULE 28 INCIDENT

A ball may be declared unplayable anywhere upon the course except in a water hazard. However, whether a ball lies in a bunker or not can have an important impact upon the player's options, as Corey Pavin discovered at the 1992 U.S. Open at Pebble Beach.

While it is a question of fact as to where a ball actually lies on the course, it sometimes takes close inspection to be certain. At the 11th hole, Pavin's ball found its way under the grassy lip of a fairway bunker. At such a position it was not readily evident whether it was in the bunker or through the green.

The definition of a bunker excludes the grass-covered ground bordering or within the hazard. The margin of the bunker extends vertically downwards but not upward, and a ball is in a bunker when it lies in or any part of it touches the bunker.

By asking for a ruling, Pavin wanted to determine where he was permitted to drop his ball under the provisions of Rule 28 in addition to taking a stroke and distance penalty. If his ball were not in the bunker, he would be permitted to drop outside the bunker under penalty of one stroke. If his ball were in the bunker, his only dropping option would be within the bunker.

After close examination, it was ruled that the ball was in the bunker. Pavin declared it unplayable and dropped in the hazard, keeping the point where the ball lay directly between the hole and the spot on which the ball was dropped. He incurred a one penalty stroke penalty under Rule 28.

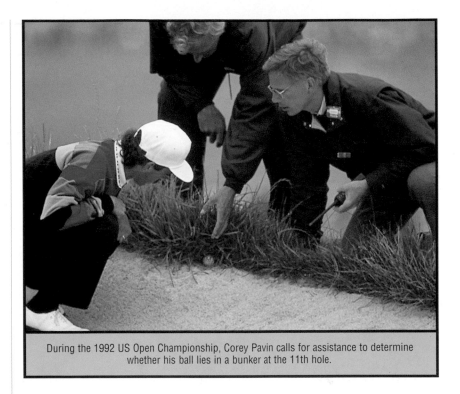

During the 1992 US Open Championship, Corey Pavin calls for assistance to determine whether his ball lies in a bunker at the 11th hole.

RULE **29**

THREESOMES AND FOURSOMES

DEFINITIONS

Threesome: A match in which one plays against two, and each side plays one ball.
Foursome: A match in which two play against two, and each side plays one ball.

See **incident** involving Rule 29 on page 121

29-1 GENERAL

In a *threesome* or a *foursome*, during any *stipulated round* the *partners* shall play alternately from the *teeing grounds* and alternately during the play of each hole. *Penalty strokes* do not affect the order of play.

29-2 MATCH PLAY

If a player plays when his partner should have played, **his side shall lose the hole**.

29-3 STROKE PLAY

If the *partners* play a *stroke* or *strokes* in incorrect order, such stroke or strokes shall be cancelled and **the side shall incur a penalty of two strokes**. The side shall correct the error by playing a ball in correct order as nearly as possible at the spot from which it first played in incorrect order (see Rule 20-5). If the side plays a stroke from the next *teeing ground* without first correcting the error or, in the case of the last hole of the round, leaves the *putting green* without declaring its intention to correct the error, **the side shall be disqualified**.

119

FOURSOMES: ORDER OF PLAY WHEN PARTNER DRIVES OUT OF BOUNDS

FOURSOMES: WHICH PARTNER DROPS BALL

Rule 29-1.
See Definition
of Stipulated
Round

RULE 29 INCIDENT

The practice putting green at the Old Course in St Andrews lies just off the course and only a few steps from the 1st tee. Paired together on the second day for the morning foursomes of the 1975 Walker Cup Match, the U.S. side of veteran William C. Campbell and newcomer John Grace reported to the tee a little ahead of time. They had already decided that Grace would drive at the odd numbered holes, so Campbell decided to use the extra time before the match began to walk to the practice green and hit a few putts.

As the visiting team, Campbell and Grace had the honour. The wind was blowing from the west off St Andrews Bay, which carried the announcement of the match's beginning beyond Campbell's earshot.

As the breeze momentarily died, Campbell heard "the click" of Grace's drive just before striking a practice putt, and he was unable to interrupt his stroke. He had practised during the play of the hole. Instantly and instinctively recognising his breach, Campbell walked onto the fairway and reported to the Referee that the U.S. had lost the first hole. [Rule 7-2 and Rule 29.]

The referee for the match accepted Campbell's report but made no immediate announcement to the other players. Because play of the hole had ended with the breach of Rule 7-2, Campbell was free to play his side's second from where Grace's good drive lay to the green, as simply more practice.

Walking across the Swilken Burn, Campbell told Grace what had taken place. "He was incredulous, to say the least," Campbell recalls.

The Americans lost the first hole and eventually lost the match to Mark James and Richard Eyles.

RULE **30**

DEFINITIONS

THREE-BALL, BEST-BALL AND FOUR-BALL MATCH PLAY

Three-Ball: A match play competition in which three play against one another, each playing his own ball. Each player is playing two distinct matches.

Best-Ball: A match in which one plays against the better ball of two or the best ball of three players.

Four-Ball: A match in which two play their better ball against the better ball of two other players.

30-1 RULES OF GOLF APPLY

The Rules of Golf, so far as they are not at variance with the following special Rules, shall apply to three-ball, best-ball and four-ball matches.

30-2 THREE-BALL MATCH PLAY

a Ball at Rest Moved by an Opponent

Except as otherwise provided in the *Rules*, if the player's ball is touched or *moved* by an opponent, his *caddie* or *equipment* other than during search, Rule 18-3b applies. **That opponent shall incur a penalty stroke in his match with the player**, but not in his match with the other opponent.

b Ball Deflected or Stopped by an Opponent Accidentally

If a player's ball is accidentally deflected or stopped by an opponent, his *caddie* or *equipment*, no penalty shall be incurred. In his match with that opponent the player may play the ball as it lies or, before another stroke is played by either side, he may cancel the stroke and play a ball without penalty as nearly as possible at the spot from which the original ball was last

BREACH OF RULE BY ONE PARTNER IN MATCH PLAY

I'll just remove this twig.

I'm afraid you're disqualified from the hole for removing a loose impediment from the bunker.
Fortunately, although I'm in the same bunker I'm not penalised because your breach of Rule 13-4 did not assist my play.

THREE-BALL MATCH PLAY	FOUR-BALL: ONE PLAYER MAY REPRESENT SIDE

Your partner's late. Are you disqualified, or just your partner?

Fortunately, neither of us. Because this is a four-ball match I am entitled to represent the side. Let's start. My partner is allowed to join us later, at the conclusion of a hole.

A John, my ball has struck your cart. What do I do now?
B In your match with me you may either play the ball as it lies or cancel that stroke and replay it. In your match with Jim you must play your original ball as it lies.
A That means I'm going to have two balls in play at the same time.
B That's right. Rule 30-2b.

played (see Rule 20-5). In his match with the other opponent, the ball shall be played as it lies.

Exception: Ball striking person attending flagstick — see Rule 17-3b.

(Ball purposely deflected or stopped by an opponent — see Rule 1-2.)

30-3 BEST-BALL AND FOUR-BALL MATCH PLAY
a Representation of Side
A side may be represented by one *partner* for all or any part of a match; all partners need not be present. An absent partner may join a match between holes, but not during play of a hole.

b Maximum of Fourteen Clubs
The side shall be penalised for a breach of Rule 4-4 by any partner.

c Order of Play
Balls belonging to the same side may be played in the order the side considers best.

d Wrong Ball
If a player plays a *stroke* with a *wrong ball* except in a *hazard*, **he shall be disqualified for that hole**, but his *partner* incurs no penalty even if the wrong ball belongs to him. If the wrong ball belongs to another player, its owner shall place a ball on the spot from which the wrong ball was first played.

e Disqualification of Side
(i)   **A side shall be disqualified** for a breach of any of the following by any *partner*:

123

Rule 1-3	Agreement to Waive Rules.
Rule 4-1 or -2	Clubs.
Rule 5-1 or -2	The Ball.
Rule 6-2a	Handicap (playing off higher handicap).
Rule 6-4	Caddie.
Rule 6-7	Undue Delay; Slow Play (repeated offence).
Rule 14-3	Artificial Devices and Unusual Equipment.

(ii) **A side shall be disqualified** for a breach of any of the following by all *partners*:

Rule 6-3	Time of Starting and Groups.
Rule 6-8	Discontinuance of Play.

f Effects of Other Penalties

If a player's breach of a *Rule* assists his *partner's* play or adversely affects an opponent's play, **the partner incurs the applicable penalty in addition to any penalty incurred by the player**.

In all other cases where a player incurs a penalty for breach of a Rule, the penalty shall not apply to his partner. Where the penalty is stated to be loss of hole, the effect shall be to disqualify the player for that hole.

g Another Form of Match Played Concurrently

In a best-ball or four-ball match when another form of match is played concurrently, the above special Rules shall apply.

RULE

FOUR-BALL STROKE PLAY

In four-ball stroke play two competitors play as *partners*, each playing his own ball. The lower score of the partners is the score for the hole. If one partner fails to complete the play of a hole, there is no penalty.

31-1 RULES OF GOLF APPLY

The Rules of Golf, so far as they are not at variance with the following special Rules, shall apply to four-ball stroke play.

31-2 REPRESENTATION OF SIDE

A *side* may be represented by either *partner* for all or any part of a *stipulated round*; both partners need not be present. An absent competitor may join his partner between holes, but not during play of a hole.

31-3 MAXIMUM OF FOURTEEN CLUBS

The *side* shall be penalised for a breach of Rule 4-4 by either *partner*.

31-4 SCORING

The *marker* is required to record for each hole only the gross score of whichever *partner's* score is to count. The gross scores to count must be individually identifiable; otherwise **the *side* shall be disqualified**. Only one

FOUR BALL STROKE PLAY

Date _3RD APRIL 1996_

Competition _SPRING OPEN FOUR-BALL_

PLAYER A _J. SUTHERLAND_ Handicap _16_ Strokes _12_

PLAYER B _W.B. TAYLOR_ Handicap _12_ Strokes _9_

Hole	Length Yards	Par	Stroke Index	Gross Score A	Gross Score B	Net Score A	Net Score B	Won X Lost– Half O	Mar. Score
1	437	4	4				3		
2	320	4	14		4		4		
3	162	3	18		4		4		
4	504	5	7	6		5			
5	181	3	16	4		4			
6	443	4	2		5		4		
7	390	4	8		5		4		
8	346	4	12	5		4			
9	340	4	10	4		3			
Out	3123	35					35		

Hole	Length Yards	Par	Stroke Index	Gross Score A	Gross Score B	Net Score A	Net Score B	Won X Lost– Half O	Mar. Score
10	425	4	3		5		4		
11	141	3	17	3		3			
12	476	5	9	6		5			
13	211	3	11		4		4		
14	437	4	5		5		4		
15	460	4	1		5		4		
16	176	3	15	4		4			
17	340	4	13		4		4		
18	435	4	6	6		5			
In	3101	34					37		
Out	3123	35					35		
T'tl	6224	69					72		
Handicap									
Net Score									

Player's Signature _J. Sutherland_

Marker's Signature _R.J. Parker_

PARTNER'S SCORES TO BE INDIVIDUALLY IDENTIFIED

1. The lower score of the partners is the score for the hole(Rule 31)

2. Only one of the partners need be responsible for complying with Rule 6-6b i.e. recording scores, checking scores, countersigning and returning the card (Rule 31-4).

3. The competitor is solely responsible for the correctness of the gross score recorded. Although there is no objection to the competitor (or his marker) entering the net score, it is the Committee's responsibility to record the better ball score for each hole, to add up the scores and to apply the handicaps recorded on the card (Rule 33-5). Thus there is no penalty for an error by the competitor (or his marker) for recording an incorrect net score.

4. Scores of the two partners must be kept in separate columns otherwise it is impossible for the Committee to apply the correct handicap. If the scores of both partners, having different handicaps, are recorded in the same column, the Committee has no alternative but to disqualify both partners (Rules 31-7 and 6-6 apply).

5. The Committee is responsible for laying down the conditions under which a competition is to be played (Rule 33-1), including the method of handicapping. In the above illustration the Committee laid down that ¾ handicaps would apply.

of the partners need be responsible for complying with Rule 6-6b. (Wrong score — see Rule 31-7a.)

31-5 ORDER OF PLAY

Balls belonging to the same *side* may be played in the order the side considers best.

31-6 WRONG BALL

If a competitor plays a *stroke* or strokes with a *wrong ball* except in a *hazard*, **he shall add two penalty strokes to his score for the hole** and shall then play the correct ball. His *partner* incurs no penalty even if the wrong ball belongs to him.

   If the wrong ball belongs to another competitor, its owner shall place a ball on the spot from which the wrong ball was first played.

31-7 DISQUALIFICATION PENALTIES

a Breach by One Partner

A *side* shall be disqualified from the competition for a breach of any of the following by either *partner*:

Rule 1-3	Agreement to Waive Rules.
Rule 3-4	Refusal to Comply with Rule.
Rule 4-1 or -2	Clubs.
Rule 5-1 or -2	The Ball.
Rule 6-2b	Handicap (playing off higher handicap; failure to record handicap).
Rule 6-4	Caddie.
Rule 6-6b	Signing and Returning Card.
Rule 6-6d	Wrong Score for Hole, i.e. when the recorded score of the partner whose score is to count is lower the actually taken. If the recorded score of the partner whose score is to count is higher than actually taken, it must stand as returned.
Rule 6-7	Undue Delay; Slow Play (repeated offence).
Rule 7-1	Practice Before or Between Rounds.
Rule 14-3	Artificial Devices and Unusual Equipment.
Rule 31-4	Gross Scores to Count Not Individually Identifiable.

b Breach by Both Partners

A *side* shall be disqualified:

(i)   for a breach by both *partners* of Rule 6-3 (Time of Starting and Groups) or Rule 6-8 (Discontinuance of Play), or

(ii) if, at the same hole, each *partner* is in breach of a *Rule* the penalty for which is disqualification from the competition or for a hole.

c For the Hole Only

In all other cases where a breach of a *Rule* would entail disqualification, **the competitor shall be disqualified only for the hole at which the breach occurred.**

31-8 EFFECT OF OTHER PENALTIES

If a competitor's breach of a *Rule* assists his *partner's* play, **the partner incurs the applicable penalty in addition to any penalty incurred by the competitor**.

In all other cases where a competitor incurs a penalty for breach of a Rule, the penalty shall not apply to his partner.

RULE 32 — BOGEY, PAR AND STABLEFORD COMPETITIONS

32-1 CONDITIONS

Bogey, par and Stableford competitions are forms of stroke competition in which play is against a fixed score at each hole. The Rules for stroke play, so far as they are not at variance with the following special Rules, apply.

a Bogey and Par Competitions

The reckoning for bogey and par competitions is made as in match play. Any hole for which a competitor makes no return shall be regarded as a loss. The winner is the competitor who is most successful in the aggregate of holes.

The *marker* is responsible for marking only the gross number of strokes for each hole where the competitor makes a net score equal to or less than the fixed score.

Note 1: Maximum of 14 Clubs — Penalties as in match play — see Rule 4-4.
Note 2: Undue Delay; Slow Play (Rule 6-7) — The competitor's score shall be adjusted by deducting one hole from the overall result.

b Stableford Competitions

The reckoning in Stableford competitions is made by points awarded in relation to a fixed score at each hole as follows:

Hole Played in	Points
More than one over fixed score or no score returned	0
One over fixed score	1
Fixed Score	2
One under fixed score	3
Two under fixed score	4
Three under fixed score	5
Four under fixed score	6

The winner is the competitor who scores the highest number of points.

The *marker* shall be responsible for marking only the gross number of strokes at each hole where the competitor's net score earns one or more points.

Note 1: Maximum of 14 Clubs (Rule 4-4) — Penalties applied as follows: From total points scored for the round, deduction of two points for each hole at which any breach occurred; maximum deduction per round: four points.
Note 2: Undue Delay; Slow Play (Rule 6-7) — The competitor's score shall be adjusted by deducting two points from the points total scored for the round.

32-2 DISQUALIFICATION PENALTIES
a From the Competition
A competitor shall be disqualified from the competition for a breach of any of the following:

Rule 1-3	Agreement to Waive Rules.
Rule 3-4	Refusal to Comply with Rule.
Rule 4-1 or -2	Clubs.
Rule 5-1 or -2	The Ball.
Rule 6-2b	Handicap (playing off higher handicap; failure to record handicap).
Rule 6-3	Time of Starting and Groups.
Rule 6-4	Caddie.
Rule 6-6b	Signing and Returning Card.
Rule 6-6d	Wrong Score for Hole, except that no penalty shall be incurred when a breach of this Rule does not affect the result of the hole.
Rule 6-7	Undue Delay; Slow Play (repeated offence).
Rule 6-8	Discontinuance of Play.
Rule 7-1	Practice Before or Between Rounds.
Rule 14-3	Artificial Devices and Unusual Equipment.

b For a Hole
In all other cases where a breach of a *Rule* would entail disqualification, **the competitor shall be disqualified only for the hole at which the breach occurred**.

RULE

See **incident** involving Rule 33-1 on page 131

THE COMMITTEE

33-1 CONDITIONS; WAIVING RULE
The *Committee* shall lay down the conditions under which a competition is to be played.

The Committee has no power to waive a Rule of Golf.

Certain special rules governing stroke play are so substantially different from those governing match play that combining the two forms of play is not practicable and is not permitted. The results of matches played and the scores returned in these circumstances shall not be accepted.

In stroke play the Committee may limit a *referee's* duties.

33-2 THE COURSE
a Defining Bounds and Margins
The *Committee* shall define accurately:
(i)   the *course* and *out of bounds*,
(ii) the margins of *water hazards* and *lateral water hazards*,
(iii) *ground under repair*, and
(iv) *obstructions* and integral parts of the course.

b New Holes

New *holes* should be made on the day on which a stroke competition begins and at such other times as the *Committee* considers necessary, provided all competitors in a single round play with each hole cut in the same position.

Exception: When it is impossible for a damaged *hole* to be repaired so that it conforms with the Definition, the *Committee* may make a new hole in a nearby similar position.

Note: Where a single round is to be played on more than one day, the *Committee* may provide in the conditions of a competition that the *holes* and *teeing grounds* may be differently situated on each day of the competition, provided that, on any one day, all competitors play with each hole and each teeing ground in the same position.

c Practice Ground

Where there is no practice ground available outside the area of a competition *course*, the *Committee* should lay down the area on which players may practice on any day of a competition, if it is practicable to do so. On any day of a stroke competition, the Committee should not normally permit practice on or to a *putting green* or from a *hazard* of the competition course.

d Course Unplayable

If the *Committee* or its authorised representative considers that for any reason the *course* is not in a playable condition or that there are circumstances which render the proper playing of the game impossible, it may, in match play or stroke play, order a temporary suspension of play or, in stroke play, declare play null and void and cancel all scores for the round in question. When a round is cancelled, all penalties incurred in that round are cancelled.

(Procedure in discontinuing and resuming play — see Rule 6-8.)

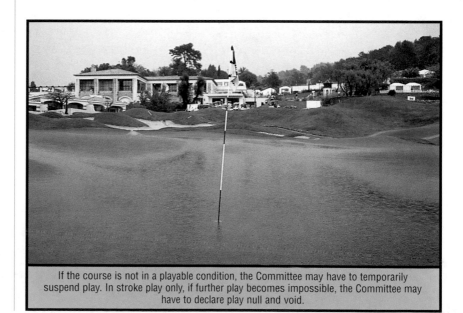

If the course is not in a playable condition, the Committee may have to temporarily suspend play. In stroke play only, if further play becomes impossible, the Committee may have to declare play null and void.

33-3 TIMES OF STARTING AND GROUPS

The *Committee* shall lay down the times of starting and, in stroke play, arrange the groups in which competitors shall play.

When a match play competition is played over an extended period, the Committee shall lay down the limit of time within which each round shall be completed. When players are allowed to arrange the date of their match within these limits, the Committee should announce that the match must be played at a stated time on the last day of the period unless the players agree to a prior date.

33-4 HANDICAP STROKE TABLE

The *Committee* shall publish a table indicating the order of holes at which handicap strokes are to be given or received.

33-5 SCORE CARD

In stroke play, the Committee shall issue for each competitor a score card containing the date and the competitor's name or, in foursome or four-ball stroke play, the competitors' names.

In stroke play, the Committee is responsible for the addition of scores and application of the handicap recorded on the card.

In four-ball stroke play, the Committee is responsible for recording the better-ball score for each hole and in the process applying the handicaps recorded on the card, and adding the better-ball scores.

In bogey, par and Stableford competitions, the Committee is responsible for applying the handicap recorded on the card and determining the result of each hole and the overall result or points total.

33-6 DECISION OF TIES

The *Committee* shall announce the manner, day and time for the decision of a halved match or of a tie, whether played on level terms or under handicap.

A halved match shall not be decided by stroke play. A tie in stroke play shall not be decided by a match.

33-7 DISQUALIFICATION PENALTY; COMMITTEE DISCRETION

A penalty of disqualification may in exceptional individual cases be waived, modified or imposed if the *Committee* considers such action warranted.

Any penalty less than disqualification shall not be waived or modified.

33-8 LOCAL RULES
a Policy

See **incident** involving Rule 33-8 on page 131

The *Committee* may make and publish Local Rules for local abnormal conditions if they are consistent with the policy set forth in Appendix I.

b Waiving or Modifying a Rule

A Rule of Golf shall not be waived by a Local Rule. However, if a *Committee* considers that local abnormal conditions interfere with the proper playing of the game to the extent that it is necessary to make a Local Rule which modifies the Rules of Golf, the Local Rule must be authorised by the Royal and Ancient Golf Club of St. Andrews.

RULE 33 INCIDENTS

Nick Faldo learned the hard way that it is always a good idea to ascertain which Local Rules have been adopted for a competition and, just as importantly, which have not.

The Royal and Ancient Golf Club of St. Andrews and the PGA European Tour have for years employed in their championships a Local Rule allowing the removal of stones in bunkers by declaring the stones to be movable obstructions. Faldo was accustomed to playing under such a Local Rule.

In the autumn of 1994, however, he ran into trouble in a bunker during the third round of the Alfred Dunhill Masters in Bali. Believing erroneously that the removal of stones was sanctioned in the Bali event as it was on the European tour, Faldo employed the Local Rule during the third round.

On the following day, a competitor was almost penalised for removing a stone in a bunker. The player's confusion stemmed from the fact that Faldo had removed a stone from a bunker the previous day.

Leading the tournament by six strokes with just six holes remaining, Faldo was called off the course. The three-time Open Champion and two-time Masters Champion had, of course, returned his score card for the third round and as it did not include the two penalty strokes for his breach of Rule 13-4, he was disqualified.

In the 3rd round of the 2000 Weetabix Women's British Open Championship at Royal Birkdale Golf Club, Karrie Webb took incorrect relief from a fixed sprinkler head on her line of play.

Webb was entitled to relief from the fixed sprinkler head within two club-lengths of the putting green by a Local Rule and together with her fellow-competitor, Trish Johnson, Webb referred to the wording of the Local Rule contained in Appendix I of the Rules of Golf. Having read the Local Rule Webb confirmed that she was entitled to relief. She determined her nearest point of relief but then mistakenly measured a one club-length area within which to drop the ball. Webb was required to drop at the nearest point of relief and having dropped and played the ball from within one club-length of this point point rather than at it, Webb was in breach of the Local Rule and incurred a penalty of two strokes.

Rules officials in the Championship office noticed the infringement on the television coverage but could not prevent the breach occurring. Webb was advised of the infringement and resulting penalty at the conclusion of her round but before she signed her score card, thereby avoiding a disqualification for signing for a score lower than actually taken.

RULE **34**

DISPUTES AND DECISIONS

34-1 CLAIMS AND PENALTIES
a Match Play

In match play if a claim is lodged with the *Committee* under Rule 2-5, a decision should be given as soon as possible so that the state of the match may, if necessary, be adjusted.

If a claim is not made within the time limit provided by Rule 2-5, it shall not be considered unless it is based on facts previously unknown to the player making the claim and the player making the claim had been given wrong information (Rules 6-2a and 9) by an opponent. In any case, no later claim shall be considered after the result of the match has been officially announced, unless the Committee is satisfied that the opponent knew he was giving wrong information.

There is no time limit on applying the disqualification penalty for a breach of Rule 1-3.

See **incident** involving Rule 34-1b on page 133

b Stroke Play

Except as provided below, in stroke play, no penalty shall be rescinded, modified or imposed after the competition has closed. A competition is deemed to have closed when the result has been officially announced or, in stroke play qualifying followed by match play, when the player has teed off in his first match.

Exceptions: A penalty of disqualification shall be imposed after the competition has closed if a competitor:

(i)   was in breach of Rule 1-3 (Agreement to Waive Rules); or

(ii)   returned a score card on which he had recorded a handicap which, before the competition closed, he knew was higher than that to which he was entitled, and this affected the number of strokes received (Rule 6-2b); or

(iii)   returned a score for any hole lower than actually taken (Rule 6-6d) for any reason other than failure to include a penalty which, before the competition closed, he did not know he had incurred; or

(iv)   knew, before the competition closed, that he had been in breach of any other *Rule* for which the prescribed penalty is disqualification.

34-2 REFEREE'S DECISION

If a *referee* has been appointed by the *Committee*, his decision shall be final.

34-3 COMMITTEE'S DECISION

In the absence of a *referee*, any dispute or doubtful point on the Rules shall be referred to the *Committee*, whose decision shall be final.

If the Committee cannot come to a decision, it shall refer the dispute or doubtful point to the Rules of Golf Committee of the Royal and Ancient Golf Club of St. Andrews, whose decision shall be final.

If the dispute or doubtful point has not been referred to the Rules of Golf Committee, the player or players have the right to refer an agreed statement through the Secretary of the Club to the Rules of Golf Committee for an opinion as to the correctness of the decision given. The reply will be sent to the Secretary of the Club or Clubs concerned.

If play is conducted other than in accordance with the Rules of Golf, the Rules of Golf Committee will not give a decision on any question.

RULE 34 INCIDENT

A case involving Mark O'Meara at the 1997 Lancombe Trophy provided a good example of the operation of Rule 34-1b. Video evidence came to light a considerable time after the competition had closed which demonstrated that during the final round O'Meara, having marked and lifted his ball on the putting green, mistakenly and unknown to himself, replaced his ball in a wrong place marginally closer to the hole.

If O'Meara's error had been noticed prior to the player returning his card, O'Meara would have been penalised two strokes at the hole concerned for playing from a wrong place (Rule 20-7b). If the breach had come to light after O'Meara had returned his card, but prior to the competition closing, the Committee would have had no choice but to disqualify him under Rule 6-6d as his score for the hole was lower than actually taken due to failure to include the penalty.

However, Rule 34-1b provides that except in the four situations listed under the Rule, the Committee may not impose, rescind or modify a penalty after the competition has closed and, as O'Meara's mistake came to light after the result of the competition had been announced this meant that no penalty was imposed by the Committee. The results stood as played, with O'Meara the winner of the Tournament by one stroke.

APPENDIX I

LOCAL RULES; CONDITIONS OF THE COMPETITION

PART A: LOCAL RULES

As provided in Rule 33-8a, the Committee may make and publish Local Rules for local abnormal conditions if they are consistent with the policy set forth in this Appendix. In addition, detailed information regarding acceptable and prohibited Local Rules is provided in "Decisions on the Rules of Golf" under Rule 33-8.

If local abnormal conditions interfere with the proper playing of the game and the Committee considers it necessary to modify a Rule of Golf, authorisation from the Royal and Ancient Golf Club of St. Andrews must be obtained.

1 DEFINING BOUNDS AND MARGINS

Specifying means used to define out of bounds, water hazards, lateral water hazards, ground under repair, obstructions and integral parts of the course (Rule 33-2a).

2 WATER HAZARDS

a Lateral Water Hazards.
Clarifying the status of water hazards which may be lateral water hazards (Rule 26).

b Provisional Ball.
Permitting play of a provisional ball for a ball which may be in a water hazard of such character that if the original ball is not found, there is reasonable evidence that it is lost in the water hazard and it would be impracticable to determine whether the ball is in the hazard or to do so would unduly delay play. The ball shall be played provisionally under any of the available options under Rule 26-1 or any applicable Local Rule. In such a case, if a provisional ball is played and the original ball is in a water hazard, the player may play the original ball as it lies or continue with the provisional ball in play, but he may not proceed under Rule 26-1 with regard to the original ball.

3 AREAS OF THE COURSE REQUIRING PRESERVATION; ENVIRONMENTALLY-SENSITIVE AREAS

Assisting preservation of the course by defining areas, including turf nurseries, young plantations and other parts of the course under cultivation, as "ground under repair" from which play is prohibited.

When the Committee is required to prohibit play from environmentally-sensitive areas which are on or adjoin the course, it should make a Local Rule clarifying the relief procedure.

4 TEMPORARY CONDITIONS – MUD, EXTREME WETNESS, POOR CONDITIONS AND PROTECTION OF COURSE

a Lifting an Embedded Ball, Cleaning
Temporary conditions which might interfere with the proper playing of the game, including mud and extreme wetness, warranting relief for an embedded ball anywhere through the green or permitting lifting, cleaning and replacing a ball anywhere through the green or on a closely-mown area through the green.

b "Preferred Lies" and "Winter Rules"
Adverse conditions, including the poor condition of the course or the existence of mud, are sometimes so general, particularly during winter months, that the Committee may decide to grant relief by temporary Local Rule either to protect the course or to promote fair and pleasant play. Such Local Rule shall be withdrawn as soon as the conditions warrant.

5 OBSTRUCTIONS

a General
Clarifying the status of objects which may be obstructions (Rule 24).

Declaring any construction to be an integral part of the course and, accordingly, not an obstruction, e.g., built-up sides of teeing grounds, putting greens and bunkers (Rules 24 and 33-2a).

b Stones in Bunkers
Allowing the removal of stones in bunkers by declaring them to be "movable obstructions" (Rule 24-1).

c Roads and Paths
(i) Declaring artificial surfaces and sides of roads and paths to be integral parts of the course, or

(ii) Providing relief of the type afforded under Rule 24-2b from roads and paths not having artificial surfaces and sides if they could unfairly affect play.

d Fixed Sprinkler Heads
Providing relief from intervention by fixed sprinkler heads on or within two club-lengths of the putting green when the ball lies within two club-lengths of the sprinkler head.

e Protection of Young Trees
Providing relief for the protection of young trees.

f Temporary Obstructions
Providing relief from interference by temporary obstructions (e.g., grandstands, television cables and equipment, etc.).

6 DROPPING ZONES (BALL DROPS)
Establishing special areas on which balls may or shall be dropped when it is not feasible or practicable to proceed exactly in conformity with Rule 24-2b or 24-2c (Immovable Obstruction), Rule 25-1b or 25-1c (Abnormal Ground Conditions), Rule 25-3 (Wrong Putting Green), Rule 26-1 (Water Hazards and Lateral Water Hazards) or Rule 28 (Ball Unplayable).

PART B: SPECIMEN LOCAL RULES

Within the policy set out in Part A of this Appendix, the Committee may adopt a Specimen Local Rule by referring, on a score card or notice board, to the examples given below. However, Specimen Local Rules 3a, 3b, 3c, 6a and 6b should not be printed or referred to on a score card as they are all of limited duration.

1 AREAS OF THE COURSE REQUIRING PRESERVATION; ENVIRONMENTALLY-SENSITIVE AREAS
a Ground Under Repair; Play Prohibited
If the Committee wishes to protect any area of the course, it should declare it to be ground

A player is entitled to relief from a fixed sprinkler head (an immovable obstruction) under Rule 24-2.
If the specimen Local Rule is introduced, a player is also entitled to relief for intervention to his line of play provided:
(**a**) the fixed sprinkler head is on or within two club-lengths of the putting green; and
(**b**) the ball lies within two club-lengths of the fixed sprinkler head.

No relief

No relief No relief No relief Local rule applies Local rule applies

The Links course at Spanish Bay in California has areas of sand dunes which have been declared environmentally-sensitive. A player may not play from or enter these areas.

under repair and prohibit play from within that area. The following Local Rule is recommended: "The _____ (defined by _____) is ground under repair from which play is prohibited. If a player's ball lies in the area, or if it interferes with the player's stance or the area of his intended swing, the player must take relief under Rule 25-1.

PENALTY FOR BREACH OF LOCAL RULE:
Match play – Loss of hole; Stroke play – Two strokes."

b Environmentally-Sensitive Areas
If an appropriate authority (i.e., a Government Agency or the like) prohibits entry into and/or play from an area on or adjoining the course for environmental reasons, the Committee should make a Local Rule clarifying the relief procedure.

The Committee has some discretion in terms of whether the area is defined as ground under repair, a water hazard or out of bounds. However, it may not simply define such an area to be a water hazard if it does not meet the Definition of a "Water Hazard" and it should attempt to preserve the character of the hole.

The following Local Rule is recommended:

"1. Definition
An environmentally-sensitive area is an area so declared by an appropriate authority, entry into and/or play from which is prohibited for environmental reasons. Such an area may be defined as ground under repair, a water hazard, a lateral water hazard or out of bounds at the discretion of the Committee provided that, in the case of an environmentally-sensitive area which has been defined as a water hazard or a lateral water hazard, the area is, by Definition, a water hazard.
Note: The Committee may not declare an area to be environmentally-sensitive.

**2. Ball in Environmentally-Sensitive Area
a Ground Under Repair**
If a ball is in an environmentally-sensitive area which is defined as ground under repair, a ball must be dropped in accordance with Rule 25-1b.

If there is reasonable evidence that a ball is lost within an environmentally-sensitive area which is defined as ground under repair, the player may take relief without penalty as prescribed in Rule 25-1c.

b Water Hazards and Lateral Water Hazards

If a ball is in or there is reasonable evidence that it is lost in an environmentally-sensitive area which is defined as a water hazard or lateral water hazard, the player must, under penalty of one stroke, proceed under Rule 26-1.

Note: If a ball dropped in accordance with Rule 26 rolls into a position where the environmentally-sensitive area interferes with the player's stance or the area of his intended swing, the player must take relief as provided in Clause 3 of this Local Rule.

c Out of Bounds

If a ball is in an environmentally-sensitive area which is defined as out of bounds, the player shall play a ball, under penalty of one stroke, as nearly as possible at the spot from which the original ball was last played (see Rule 20-5).

3. Interference with Stance or Area of Intended Swing

Interference by an environmentally-sensitive area occurs when such a condition interferes with the player's stance or the area of his intended swing. If interference exists, the player must take relief as follows:

(i) **Through the Green:** If the ball lies through the green, the point on the course nearest to where the ball lies shall be determined which (a) is not nearer the hole, (b) avoids interference by the condition and (c) is not in a hazard or on a putting green. The player shall lift the ball and drop it without penalty within one club-length of the point thus determined on a part of the course that fulfils (a), (b) and (c) above.

(ii) **In a Hazard:** If the ball is in a hazard, the player shall lift the ball and drop it either:
(a) Without penalty, in the hazard, as near as possible to the spot where the ball lay, but not nearer the hole, on a part of the course which provides complete relief from the condition; or
(b) **Under penalty of one stroke**, outside the hazard, keeping the point where the ball lay directly between the hole and the spot on which the ball is dropped, with no limit to how far behind the hazard the ball may be dropped. Additionally, the player may proceed under Rule 26 or 28 if applicable.

(iii) **On the Putting Green:** If the ball lies on the putting green, the player shall lift the ball and place it without penalty in the nearest position to where it lay which affords complete relief from the condition, but not nearer the hole or in a hazard.

The ball may be cleaned when so lifted under Clause 3 of this Local Rule.

Exception: A player may not obtain relief under Clause 3 of this Local Rule if (a) it is clearly unreasonable for him to play a stroke because of interference by anything other than a condition covered by this Local Rule or (b) interference by such a condition would occur only through use of an unnecessarily abnormal stance, swing or direction of play.

PENALTY FOR BREACH OF LOCAL RULE:
Match play – Loss of hole; Stroke play – Two strokes.

Note: In case of a serious breach of this Local Rule, the Committee may impose a penalty of disqualification."

2 PROTECTION OF YOUNG TREES

When it is desired to prevent damage to young trees, the following Local Rule is recommended:

"Protection of young trees identified by _____ . If such a tree interferes with a player's stance or the area of his intended swing, the ball must be lifted, without penalty, and dropped in accordance with the procedure prescribed in Rule 24-2b (Immovable Obstruction). If the ball lies in a water hazard, the player shall lift and drop the ball in accordance with Rule 24-2b(i) except that the nearest point of relief must be in the water hazard and the ball must be dropped in the water hazard or the player may proceed under Rule 26. The ball may be cleaned when so lifted.

Exception: A player may not obtain relief under this Local Rule if (a) it is clearly unreasonable for him to play a stroke because of interference by anything other than such tree or (b) interference by such tree would occur only through use of an unnecessarily abnormal stance, swing or direction of play.

PENALTY FOR BREACH OF LOCAL RULE:
Match play — Loss of hole; Stroke play — Two strokes."

3 TEMPORARY CONDITIONS – MUD, EXTREME WETNESS, POOR CONDITIONS AND PROTECTION OF THE COURSE

a Relief for Embedded Ball; Cleaning Ball
Rule 25-2 provides relief without penalty for a ball embedded in its own pitch-mark in any closely-mown area through the green. On the putting green, a ball may be lifted and damage caused by the impact of a ball may be repaired (Rules 16-1b and c). When permission to take relief for an embedded ball anywhere through the green would be warranted, the following Local Rule is recommended:

"Through the green, a ball which is embedded in its own pitch-mark in the ground, other than sand, may be lifted without penalty, cleaned and dropped as near as possible to where it lay but not nearer the hole. The ball when dropped must first strike a part of the course through the green.

Exception: A player may not obtain relief under this Local Rule if it is clearly unreasonable for him to play a stroke because of interference by anything other than the condition covered by this Local Rule.

PENALTY FOR BREACH OF LOCAL RULE:
Match play — Loss of hole; Stroke play — Two strokes."

Alternatively, conditions may be such that permission to lift, clean and replace the ball will suffice. In such circumstances, the following Local Rule is recommended:
"(Specify area) a ball may be lifted, cleaned and replaced without penalty.
Note: The position of the ball shall be marked before it is lifted under this Local Rule – see Rule 20-1.

PENALTY FOR BREACH OF LOCAL RULE:
Match play — Loss of hole; Stroke play — Two strokes."

b "Preferred Lies" and "Winter Rules"
The R&A does not endorse "preferred lies" or "winter rules" and recommends that the Rules of Golf be observed uniformly. Ground under

repair is provided for in Rule 25 and occasional local abnormal conditions which might interfere with fair play and are not widespread should be defined as ground under repair.

However, adverse conditions are sometimes so general throughout a course that the Committee believes "preferred lies" or "winter rules" would promote fair play or help protect the course. Heavy snows, spring thaws, prolonged rains or extreme heat can make fairways unsatisfactory and sometimes prevent use of heavy mowing equipment.

When a Committee adopts a Local Rule for "preferred lies" or "winter rules" it should be set out in detail and should be interpreted by the Committee, as there is no established code for "winter rules". Without a detailed Local Rule, it is meaningless for a Committee to post a notice merely saying "Winter Rules today."

The following Local Rule would seem appropriate for the conditions in question, but the R&A will not interpret it:

"A ball lying on a closely-mown area through the green may, without penalty, be moved or may be lifted, cleaned and placed within (specify area, e.g., six inches, one club-length, etc.) of where it originally lay, but not nearer the hole and not in a hazard or on a putting green. A player may move or place his ball once and after the ball has been so moved or placed, it is in play.

PENALTY FOR BREACH OF LOCAL RULE:
Match play – Loss of hole; Stroke play – Two strokes."

Before a Committee adopts a Local Rule permitting "preferred lies" or "winter rules", the following facts should be considered:

1. Such a Local Rule conflicts with the Rules of Golf and the fundamental principle of playing the ball as it lies.
2. "Winter rules" are sometimes adopted under the guise of protecting the course when, in fact, the practical effect is just the opposite – they permit moving the ball to the best turf, from which divots are then taken to injure the course further.
3. "Preferred lies" or "winter rules" tend generally to lower scores and handicaps, thus penalising the players in competition with players whose scores for handicaps are made under the Rules of Golf.
4. Extended use or indiscriminate use of "preferred lies" or "winter rules" will place players at a disadvantage when competing at a course where the ball must be played as it lies.

c Aeration Holes

When a course has been aerated, a Local Rule permitting relief, without penalty, from an aeration hole may be warranted. The following Local Rule is recommended:

"Through the green, a ball which comes to rest in or on an aeration hole may be lifted without penalty, cleaned and dropped, as near as possible to the spot where it lay but not nearer the hole. The ball when dropped must first strike a part of the course through the green.

On the putting green, the player shall place the ball at the nearest spot not nearer the hole which avoids such situation.

PENALTY FOR BREACH OF LOCAL RULE:
Match play – Loss of hole; Stroke play – Two strokes."

4 STONES IN BUNKERS

Stones are, by Definition, loose impediments and, when a player's ball is in a hazard, a stone lying in or touching the hazard may not be touched or moved (Rule 13-4). However, stones in bunkers may represent a danger to players (a player could be injured by a stone struck by the player's club in an attempt to play the ball) and they may interfere with the proper playing of the game.

When permission to lift a stone in a bunker would be warranted, the following Local Rule is recommended:
"Stones in bunkers are movable obstructions (Rule 24-1 applies)."

5 FIXED SPRINKLER HEADS

Rule 24-2 provides relief without penalty from interference by an immovable obstruction, but it also provides that, except on the putting green, intervention on the line of play is not, of itself, interference under this Rule.

However, on some courses, the aprons of the

putting greens are so closely mown that players may wish to putt from just off the green. In such conditions, fixed sprinkler heads on the apron may interfere with the proper playing of the game and the introduction of the following Local Rule providing additional relief without penalty from intervention by a fixed sprinkler head would be warranted:

"All fixed sprinkler heads are immovable obstructions and relief from interference by them may be obtained under Rule 24-2. In addition, if a ball lies off the putting green but not in a hazard and such an obstruction on or within two club-lengths of the putting green and within two club-lengths of the ball intervenes on the line of play between the ball and the hole, the player may take relief as follows:

The ball shall be lifted and dropped at the nearest point to where the ball lay which (a) is not nearer the hole, (b) avoids such intervention and (c) is not in a hazard or on a putting green. The ball may be cleaned when so lifted.

PENALTY FOR BREACH OF LOCAL RULE:
Match play — Loss of hole; Stroke play — Two strokes."

6 TEMPORARY OBSTRUCTIONS

When temporary obstructions are installed on or adjoining the course, the Committee should define the status of such obstructions as movable, immovable or temporary immovable obstructions.

a Temporary Immovable Obstructions

If the Committee defines such obstructions as temporary immovable obstructions, the following Local Rule is recommended:

"1. Definition

A temporary immovable obstruction is a non-permanent artificial object which is often erected in conjunction with a competition and which is fixed or not readily movable.

Examples of temporary immovable obstructions include, but are not limited to, tents, scoreboards, grandstands, television towers and lavatories.

Supporting guy wires are part of the temporary immovable obstruction unless the Committee declares that they are to be treated as elevated power lines or cables.

2. Interference

Interference by a temporary immovable obstruction occurs when (a) the ball lies in front of and so close to the obstruction that the obstruction interferes with the player's stance or the area of his intended swing, or (b) the ball lies in, on, under or behind the obstruction so that any part of the obstruction intervenes directly between the player's ball and the hole; interference also exists if the ball lies within one club-length of a spot where such intervention would exist.

Note: A ball is under a temporary immovable obstruction when it is below the outer most edges of the obstruction, even if these edges do not extend downwards to the ground.

3. Relief

A player may obtain relief from interference by a temporary immovable obstruction, including a temporary immovable obstruction which is out of bounds, as follows:

(a) **Through the Green:** If the ball lies through the green, the point on the course nearest to where the ball lies shall be determined which (a) is not nearer the hole, (b) avoids interference as defined in Clause 2 and (c) is not in a hazard or on a putting green. The player shall lift the ball and drop it without penalty within one club-length of the point thus determined on a part of the course which fulfils (a), (b) and (c) above.

(b) **In a Hazard:** If the ball is in a hazard, the player shall lift and drop the ball either:

(i)   Without penalty, in the hazard, on the nearest part of the course affording complete relief within the limits specified in Clause 3a above or, if complete relief is impossible, on a part of the course within the hazard which affords maximum available relief; or

(ii) Under the penalty of one stroke, outside the hazard as follows: the point on the course nearest to where the ball lies shall be determined which (a) is not nearer the hole, (b) avoids interference as defined in

If there are temporary immovable obstructions, such as TV towers, on the course, the Committee should introduce a Local Rule providing for relief from such temporary immovable obstructions.

Clause 2 and (c) is not in a hazard. The player shall drop the ball within one club-length of the point thus determined on a part of the course which fulfils (a), (b) and (c) above.

The ball may be cleaned when lifted under Clause 3.

Note 1: If the ball lies in a hazard, nothing in this Local Rule precludes the player from proceeding under Rule 26 or Rule 28, if applicable.

Note 2: If the ball to be dropped under this Local Rule is not immediately recoverable, another ball may be substituted.

Note 3: A Committee may make a Local Rule (a) permitting or requiring a player to use a dropping zone or ball drop when taking relief from a temporary immovable obstruction or (b) permitting a player, as an additional relief option, to drop the ball on the opposite side of the obstruction from the point established under Clause 3, but otherwise in accordance with Clause 3.

Exceptions:
If a player's ball lies in front of or behind the temporary immovable obstruction (not in, on or under the obstruction) he may not obtain relief under Clause 3 if:

1. It is clearly unreasonable for him to play a stroke or, in the case of intervention, to play a stroke such that the ball could finish on a direct line to the hole, because of interference by anything other than the temporary immovable obstruction;

2. Interference by the temporary immovable obstruction would occur only through use of an unnecessarily abnormal stance, swing or direction of play; or

3. In the case of intervention, it would be clearly unreasonable to expect the player to be able to strike the ball far enough towards the hole to reach the temporary immovable obstruction.

Note: A player not entitled to relief due to these exceptions may proceed under Rule 24-2.

4. Ball Lost

If there is reasonable evidence that the ball is lost in, on or under a temporary immovable obstruction, a ball may be dropped under the provisions of Clause 3 or Clause 5, if applicable. For the purpose of applying Clauses 3 and 5, the ball shall be deemed to lie at the spot where it last entered the obstruction (Rule 24-2c).

5. Dropping Zones (Ball Drops)

If the player has interference from a temporary immovable obstruction, the Committee may permit or require the use of a dropping zone or ball drop. If the player uses a dropping zone in taking relief, he must drop the ball in the dropping zone nearest to where his ball originally lay or is deemed to lie under Clause 4 (even though the nearest dropping zone may be nearer the hole).

Note 1: A Committee may make a Local Rule prohibiting the use of a dropping zone or ball drop which is nearer the hole.

Note 2: If the ball is dropped in a dropping zone, the ball shall not be re-dropped if it comes to rest within two club-lengths of the spot where it first struck a part of the course even though it may come to rest nearer the hole or outside the boundaries of the dropping zone.

PENALTY FOR BREACH OF LOCAL RULE:
Match play – Loss of hole; Stroke play – Two strokes."

b Temporary Power Lines and Cables

When temporary power lines, cables, or telephone lines are installed on the course, the following Local Rule is recommended:

141

"Temporary power lines, cables, telephone lines and mats covering or stanchions supporting them are obstructions:
1. If they are readily movable, Rule 24-1 applies.
2. If they are fixed or not readily movable, the player may, if the ball lies through the green or in a bunker, obtain relief as provided in Rule 24-2b. If the ball lies in a water hazard, the player may lift and drop the ball in accordance with Rule 24-2b(i) except that the nearest point of relief must be in the water hazard and the ball must be dropped in the water hazard or the player may proceed under Rule 26.
3. If a ball strikes an elevated power line or cable, the stroke shall be cancelled and replayed, without penalty (see Rule 20-5). If the ball is not immediately recoverable another ball may be substituted.
   Note: Guy wires supporting a temporary immovable obstruction are part of the temporary immovable obstruction unless the Committee, by Local Rule, declares that they are to be treated as elevated power lines or cables.
   Exception: Ball striking elevated junction section of cable rising from the ground shall not be replayed.
4. Grass-covered cable trenches are ground under repair even if not so marked and Rule 25-1b applies."

PART C: CONDITIONS OF THE COMPETITION

Rule 33-1 provides, "The Committee shall lay down the conditions under which a competition is to be played." Such conditions should include many matters such as method of entry, eligibility, number of rounds to be played, etc. which it is not appropriate to deal with in the Rules of Golf or this Appendix. Detailed information regarding such conditions is provided in "Decisions on the Rules of Golf" under Rule 33-1.

However, there are seven matters which might be covered in the Conditions of the Competition to which the Committee's atten-

tion is specifically drawn by way of a Note to the appropriate Rule. These are:

1. SPECIFICATION OF THE BALL (NOTE TO RULE 5-1)

The following two conditions are recommended only for competitions involving expert players:

a List of Conforming Golf Balls

The R&A periodically issues a List of Conforming Golf Balls which list balls that have been tested and found to conform. If the Committee wishes to require use of a brand of golf ball on the List, the List should be posted and the following condition of competition used:

"The ball the player uses shall be named on the current List of Conforming Golf Balls issued by the Royal and Ancient Golf Club of St. Andrews.

PENALTY FOR BREACH OF CONDITION:
Disqualification."

b One Ball Condition

If it is desired to prohibit changing brands and types of golf balls during a stipulated round, the following condition is recommended:
"Limitation on Balls Used During Round: (Note to Rule 5-1)
(i) "One Ball" Condition
    During a stipulated round, the balls a player uses must be of the same brand and type as detailed by a single entry on the current List of Conforming Golf Balls.

PENALTY FOR BREACH OF CONDITION:
Match play — At the conclusion of the hole at which the breach is discovered, the state of the match shall be adjusted by deducting one hole for each hole at which a breach occurred; maximum deduction per round: Two holes.
Stroke play — Two strokes for each hole at which any breach occurred; maximum penalty per round: Four strokes.

(ii) Procedure When Breach Discovered
    When a player discovers that he has used a ball in breach of this condition, he shall abandon that ball before playing from the next teeing ground and complete the round using a proper ball; otherwise, the player

shall be disqualified. If discovery is made during play of a hole and the player elects to substitute a proper ball before completing that hole, the player shall place a proper ball on the spot where the ball used in breach of the condition lay."

2 TIME OF STARTING (NOTE TO RULE 6-3a)

If the Committee wishes to act in accordance with the Note, the following wording is recommended:

"If the player arrives at his starting point, ready to play, within five minutes after his starting time in the absence of circumstances which warrant waiving the penalty of disqualification as provided in Rule 33-7, the penalty for failure to start on time is loss of the first hole to be played in match play or two strokes in stroke play. Penalty for lateness beyond five minutes is disqualification."

3 PACE OF PLAY

The Committee may lay down pace of play guidelines to help prevent slow play, in accordance with Note 2 to Rule 6-7.

4 SUSPENSION OF PLAY DUE TO A DANGEROUS SITUATION (NOTE TO RULE 6-8b)

As there have been many deaths and injuries from lightning on golf courses, all clubs and sponsors of golf competitions are urged to take precautions for the protection of persons against lightning. Attention is called to Rules 6-8 and 33-2d. If the Committee desires to adopt the condition in the Note under Rule 6-8b, the following wording is recommended:

"When play is suspended by the Committee for a dangerous situation, if the players in a match or group are between the play of two holes, they shall not resume play until the Committee has ordered a resumption of play. If they are in the process of playing a hole, they shall discontinue play immediately and shall not thereafter resume play until the Committee has ordered a resumption of play. If a player fails to discontinue play immediately, he shall be disqualified unless circumstances warrant waiving such penalty as provided in Rule 33-7.

The signal for suspending play due to a dangerous situation will be a prolonged note of the siren."

SUSPENSION OF PLAY DUE TO A DANGEROUS SITUATION

The following signals are generally used and it is recommended that all Committees do similarly:

Discontinue Play Immediately: One prolonged note of siren.

Discontinue Play: Three consecutive notes of siren, repeated.

Resume Play: Two short notes of siren, repeated.

5 PRACTICE

a General

The Committee may make regulations governing practice in accordance with the Note to Rule 7-1, Exception (c) to Rule 7-2, Note 2 to Rule 7 and Rule 33-2c.

b Practice Between Holes (Note 2 to Rule 7)

It is recommended that a condition of competition prohibiting practice putting or chipping on or near the putting green of the hole last played is introduced only in stroke play competitions. The following wording is recommended:

"A player shall not play any practice stroke on or near the putting green of the hole last played. If a practice stroke is played on or near the putting green of the hole last played, the player shall incur a penalty of two strokes at the next hole, except that in the case of the last hole of the round, he incurs the penalty at that hole."

6 ADVICE IN TEAM COMPETITIONS

If the Committee wishes to act in accordance with the Note under Rule 8, the following wording is recommended:

"In accordance with the Note to Rule 8 of the Rules of Golf, each team may appoint one person (in addition to the persons from whom advice may be asked under the Rule) who may give advice to members of that team. Such person (if it is desired to insert any restriction on who may be nominated insert such restriction here) shall be identified to the Committee before giving advice."

7 NEW HOLES

The Committee may provide, in accordance with the Note to Rule 33-2b, that the holes and teeing grounds for a single round competition, being held on more than one day, may be differently situated on each day.

Other conditions of the competition might include:

TRANSPORTATION

If it is desired to require players to walk in a competition, the following condition is recommended:

"Players shall walk at all times during a stipulated round.

PENALTY FOR BREACH OF CONDITION:
Match play – At the conclusion of the hole at which the breach is discovered, the state of the match shall be adjusted by deducting one hole for each hole at which a breach occurred. Maximum deduction per round: Two holes.
Stroke play – Two strokes for each hole at which any breach occurred; maximum penalty per round: Four strokes. In the event of a breach between the play of two holes, the penalty applies to the next hole.
Match or stroke play – Use of any unauthorised form of transportation shall be discontinued immediately upon discovery that a breach has occurred. Otherwise, the player shall be disqualified."

HOW TO DECIDE TIES

Rule 33-6 empowers the Committee to determine how and when a halved match or a stroke play tie shall be decided. The decision should be published in advance.

The R&A recommends:

Match Play

A match which ends all square should be played off hole by hole until one side wins a hole. The play-off should start on the hole where the match began. In a handicap match, handicap strokes should be allowed as in the prescribed round.

Stroke Play

(a) In the event of a tie in a scratch stroke play competition, a play-off is recommended. Such a play-off may be over 18 holes or a smaller number of holes as specified by the Committee. If that is not feasible or there is still a tie, a hole-by-hole play-off is recommended.

(b) In the event of a tie in a handicap stroke play competition, a play-off with handicaps is recommended. Such a play-off may be over 18 holes or a smaller number of holes as specified by the Committee. If the play-off is less than 18 holes, the percentage of 18 holes to be played should be applied to the players' handicaps to determine their play-off handicaps. Handicap stroke fractions of one-half stroke or more should count as a full stroke and any lesser fraction should be disregarded.

(c) In either a scratch or handicap stroke play competition, if a play-off of any type is not feasible, matching score cards is recommended. The method of matching cards should be announced in advance. An acceptable method of matching cards is to determine the winner on the basis of the best score for the last nine holes. If the tying players have the same score for the last nine, determine the winner on the basis of the last six holes, last three holes and finally the 18th hole. If such a method is used in a handicap stroke play competition, one-half, one-third, one-sixth, etc. of the handicaps should be deducted.

Fractions should not be disregarded. If such a method is used in a competition with a multiple tee start, it is recommended that the "last nine holes, last six holes, etc." is considered to be holes 10-18, 13-18, etc.

(d) If the conditions of the competition provide that ties shall be decided over the last nine, last six, last three and last hole, they should also provide what will happen if this procedure does not produce a winner.

DRAW FOR MATCH PLAY

Although the draw for match play may be completely blind or certain players may be distributed through different quarters or eighths, the General Numerical Draw is recommended if matches are determined by a qualifying round.

General Numerical Draw

For purposes of determining places in the draw, ties in qualifying rounds other than those for the last qualifying place shall be decided by the order in which scores are returned, with the first score to be returned receiving the lowest available number, etc. If it is impossible to determine the order in which scores are returned, ties shall be determined by a blind draw.

UPPER HALF	LOWER HALF	UPPER HALF	LOWER HALF
64 QUALIFIERS		32 QUALIFIERS	
1 vs 64	2 vs 63	1 vs 32	2 vs 31
32 vs 33	31 vs 34	16 vs 17	15 vs 18
16 vs 49	15 vs 50	8 vs 25	7 vs 26
17 vs 48	18 vs 47	9 vs 24	10 vs 23
8 vs 57	7 vs 58	4 vs 29	3 vs 30
25 vs 40	26 vs 39	13 vs 20	14 vs 19
9 vs 56	10 vs 55	5 vs 28	6 vs 27
24 vs 41	23 vs 42	12 vs 21	11 vs 22
4 vs 61	3 vs 62	16 QUALIFIERS	
29 vs 36	30 vs 35	1 vs 16	2 vs 15
13 vs 52	14 vs 51	8 vs 9	7 vs 10
20 vs 45	19 vs 46	4 vs 13	3 vs 14
5 vs 60	6 vs 59	5 vs 12	6 vs 11
28 vs 37	27 vs 38	8 QUALIFIERS	
12 vs 53	11 vs 54	1 vs 8	2 vs 7
21 vs 44	22 vs 43	4 vs 5	3 vs 6

APPENDICES II & III

Any design in a club or ball which is not covered by Rules 4 and 5 and Appendices II and III, or which might significantly change the nature of the game, will be ruled on by the Royal and Ancient Golf Club of St. Andrews. The dimensions contained in Appendices II and III are referenced in imperial measurements. A metric conversion is also referenced for information, calculated using a conversion rate of 1 inch = 25.4 mm. In the event of any dispute over the conformity of a club or ball, the imperial measurements shall take precedence.

APPENDIX II

DESIGN OF CLUBS

A player in doubt as to the conformity of a club should consult the Royal and Ancient Golf Club of St. Andrews.

A manufacturer should submit to the Royal and Ancient Golf Club of St. Andrews a sample of a club which is to be manufactured for a ruling as to whether the club conforms with the Rules. If a manufacturer fails to submit a sample before manufacturing and/or marketing the club, the manufacturer assumes the risk of a ruling that the club does not conform with the Rules. Any sample submitted to the Royal and Ancient Golf Club of St. Andrews will become its property for reference purposes.

The following paragraphs prescribe general regulations for the design of clubs, together with specifications and interpretations.

Where a club, or part of a club, is required to have some specific property, this means that it must be designed and manufactured with the intention of having that property. The finished club or part must have that property within manufacturing tolerances appropriate to the material used.

1 CLUBS
a General
A club is an implement designed to be used for striking the ball and generally comes in three forms: woods, irons and putters distinguished by shape and intended use. A putter is a club with a loft not exceeding ten degrees designed primarily for use on the putting green.

The club shall not be substantially different from the traditional and customary form and make. The club shall be composed of a shaft and a head. All parts of the club shall be fixed so that the club is one unit, and it shall have no external attachments except as otherwise permitted by the *Rules*.

b Adjustability
Woods and irons shall not be designed to be adjustable except for weight. Putters may be designed to be adjustable for weight and some other forms of adjustability are also permitted. All methods of adjustment permitted by the *Rules* require that:
(i)   the adjustment cannot be readily made;
(ii) all adjustable parts are firmly fixed and there is no reasonable likelihood of them working loose during a round; and
(iii) all configurations of adjustment conform with the Rules.
The disqualification penalty for purposely changing the playing characteristics of a club during a *stipulated round* (Rule 4-2a) applies to all clubs including a putter.

c Length
The overall length of the club shall be at least 18 inches (457.2mm) measured from the top of the grip along the axis of the shaft or a straight line extension of it to the sole of the club.

d Alignment

When the club is in its normal address position the shaft shall be so aligned that:

(i) the projection of the straight part of the shaft on to the vertical plane through the toe and heel shall diverge from the vertical by at least 10 degrees (see Fig. I);

(ii) the projection of the straight part of the shaft on to the vertical plane along the intended line of play shall not diverge from the vertical by more than 20 degrees (see Fig. II).

Except for putters, all of the heel portion of the club shall lie within 0.625 inches (15.88 mm) of the plane containing the axis of the straight part of the shaft and the intended (horizontal) line of play (see Fig. III).

2 SHAFT

a Straightness

The shaft shall be straight from the top of the grip to a point not more than 5 inches (127 mm) above the sole, measured from the point where the shaft ceases to be straight along the axis of the bent part of the shaft and the neck and/or socket (see Fig. IV).

b Bending and Twisting Properties

At any point along its length, the shaft shall:

(i) bend in such a way that the deflection is the same regardless of how the shaft is rotated about its longitudinal axis; and

(ii) twist the same amount in both directions.

c Attachment to Clubhead

The shaft shall be attached to the clubhead at the heel either directly or through a single plain neck and/or socket. The length from the top of the neck and/or socket to the sole of the club shall not exceed 5 inches (127mm), measured along the axis of, and following any bend in, the neck and/or socket (see Fig. V).

Exception for Putters: The shaft or neck or socket of a putter may be fixed at any point in the head.

3 GRIP (SEE FIG. VI)

The grip consists of material added to the shaft to enable the player to obtain a firm hold. The grip shall be straight and plain in form, shall extend to the end of the shaft and shall not be molded for any part of the hands. If no material is added, that portion of the shaft designed to be held by the player shall be considered the grip.

(i) For clubs other than putters the grip must be circular in cross-section, except that a continuous, straight, slightly raised rib may be incorporated along the full length of the grip, and a slightly indented spiral is permitted on a wrapped grip or a replica of one.

(ii) A putter grip may have a non-circular cross-section, provided the cross-section has no concavity, is symmetrical and remains generally similar throughout the length of the grip. (See Clause (v) below).

(iii) The grip may be tapered but must not have any bulge or waist. Its cross-sectional dimensions measured in any direction must not exceed 1.75 inches (44.45mm).

(iv) For clubs other than putters the axis of the grip must coincide with the axis of the shaft.

(v) A putter may have two grips provided each is circular in cross-section, the axis of each coincides with the axis of the shaft, and they are separated by at least 1.5 inches (38.1mm).

4 CLUBHEAD

a Plain in Shape

The clubhead shall be generally plain in shape. All parts shall be rigid, structural in nature and functional. It is not practicable to define plain in shape precisely and comprehensively but features which are deemed to be in breach of this requirement and are therefore not permitted include:

(i) holes through the head,

(ii) transparent material added for other than decorative or structural purposes,

(iii) appendages to the main body of the head such as knobs, plates, rods or fins, for the purpose of meeting dimensional

FIG VI

Circular cross-section

Non circular cross-section (putters only)

Waist (not permitted)

Bulge (not permitted)

FIG IX

Face Back Toe Heel .625" A B

FIG VII

Illustrative impact area

FIG VIII

Axis of symmetry Groove width (max .035") Groove depth (max .020") 30° 30°

Examples of permissible groove cross-sections

specifications, for aiming or for any other purpose. Exceptions may be made for putters.

Any furrows in or runners on the sole shall not extend into the face.

b Dimensions

The distance from the heel to the toe of the clubhead shall be greater than the distance from the face to the back. These dimensions are measured, with the clubhead in its normal address position, on horizontal lines between vertical projections of the outermost points of (i) the heel and the toe and (ii) the face and the back (see Fig. VII, dimension A). If the outermost point of the heel is not clearly defined, it is deemed to be 0.625 inches (15.88mm) above the horizontal plane on which the club is resting in its normal address position (see Fig. VII, dimension B).

c Striking Faces

The clubhead shall only have one striking face, except that a putter may have two such faces if their characteristics are the same, and they are opposite each other.

5 CLUB FACE

a General

The material and construction of, or any treatment to, the face or clubhead shall not have the effect at impact of a spring (test on file), or impart significantly more spin to the ball than a standard steel face, or have any other effect which would unduly influence the movement of the ball.

The face of the club shall be hard and rigid (some exceptions may be made for putters) and, except for such markings listed below, shall be smooth and shall not have any degree of concavity.

b Impact Area Roughness and Material

Except for markings specified in the following paragraphs, the surface roughness within the area where impact is intended (the "impact

149

area") must not exceed that of decorative sandblasting, or of fine milling (see Fig. VIII).

The whole of the impact area must be of the same material. Exceptions may be made for wooden clubs.

c Impact Area Markings

Markings in the impact area must not have sharp edges or raised lips as determined by a finger test. Grooves or punch marks in the impact area must meet the following specifications:

(i) **Grooves.** A series of straight grooves with diverging sides and a symmetrical cross-section may be used (see Fig. IX). The width and cross-section must be consistent across the face of the club and along the length of the grooves. Any rounding of groove edges shall be in the form of a radius which does not exceed 0.020 inches (0.508 mm). The width of the grooves shall not exceed 0.035 inches (0.9mm), using the 30 degree method of measurement on file with the Royal and Ancient Golf Club of St. Andrews. The distance between edges of adjacent grooves must not be less than three times the width of a groove, and not less than 0.075 inches (1.905mm). The depth of a groove must not exceed 0.020 inches (0.508mm).

(ii) **Punch Marks.** Punch marks may be used. The area of any such mark must not exceed 0.0044 square inches (2.84 sq. mm). A mark must not be closer to an adjacent mark than 0.168 inches (4.27 mm) measured from center to center. The depth of a punch mark must not exceed 0.040 inches (1.02 mm). If punch marks are used in combination with grooves, a punch mark must not be closer to a groove than 0.168 inches (4.27 mm), measured from center to center.

d Decorative Markings

The center of the impact area may be indicated by a design within the boundary of a square whose sides are 0.375 inches (9.53 mm) in length. Such a design must not unduly influence the movement of the ball. Decorative markings are permitted outside the impact area.

e Non-metallic Club Face Markings

The above specifications apply to clubs on which the impact area of the face is of metal or a material of similar hardness. They do not apply to clubs with faces made of other materials and whose loft angle is 24 degrees or less, but markings which could unduly influence the movement of the ball are prohibited. Clubs with this type of face and a loft angle exceeding 24 degrees may have grooves of maximum width 0.040 inches (1.02 mm) and maximum depth 1½ times the groove width, but must otherwise conform to the markings specifications above.

f Putter Face

The specifications above with regard to roughness, material and markings in the impact area do not apply to putters.

APPENDIX III

THE BALL

1 WEIGHT
The weight of the ball shall not be greater than 1.620 ounces avoirdupois (45.93 gm).

2 SIZE
The diameter of the ball shall be not less than 1.680 inches (42.67mm). This specification will be satisfied if, under its own weight, a ball falls through a 1.680 inches diameter ring gauge in fewer than 25 out of 100 randomly selected positions, the test being carried out at a temperature of 23 ± 1°C.

3 SPHERICAL SYMMETRY
The ball must not be designed, manufactured or intentionally modified to have properties which differ from those of a spherically symmetrical ball.

4 INITIAL VELOCITY
The initial velocity of the ball shall not exceed the limit specified (test on file) when measured on apparatus approved by the Royal and Ancient Golf Club of St. Andrews.

5 OVERALL DISTANCE STANDARD
The combined carry and roll of the ball, when tested on apparatus approved by the Royal and Ancient Golf Club of St. Andrews, shall not exceed the distance specified under the conditions set forth in the Overall Distance Standard for golf balls on file with the Royal and Ancient Golf Club of St. Andrews.

HANDICAPS

The Rules of Golf do not legislate for the allocation and adjustment of handicaps. Such matters are within the jurisdiction of the National Union concerned and queries should be directed accordingly.

PHOTOGRAPHIC ACKNOWLEDGEMENTS

Allsport 98 top left, /David Cannon 12, 30, 42, 76, 87 top,
115, 119, /Graham Chadwick 109 bottom, /Phil Cole 129,
/Stephen Dunn 47, 55, /David Frost 92, /Craig Jones 87
bottom, /Warren Little 44, /Stephen Munday 7 bottom,
105, /Andrew Redington 30 bottom, 31, 35
Peter Dazeley 23 left, 98 top right
Joann Dost Golf Editions /Joann Dost 68 bottom
Hulton Getty Picture Collection 19
Phil Sheldon Golf Picture Library 7 top, 23 right, 50 top,
59, 97, 106, 136, 141
United States Golf Association 27 bottom